bant eu angeli dicentes . Surge tol[
uxore tua · z duas filias n̄s h[...].n[
z tu pariter p̄a[...]
simulante illo : [...] e[
et manū uxoris [...] e[
cp parceret dn̄s i [...]uq; eū z p[
suerūt extra ciuitate · ibiq; locuti sun[
ad eum dicentes . Salua animā tu[
Noli respicere post tergum · nec stes i[
omni loco circa regione · sed ī mont[
saluū te fac · ne z tu simul p̄as . Dix[
q; loch ad eos . Queso dn̄e mi · qui[
inuenit seruus tu⁹ g̃ñā corā te · et m[
gnificasti gloriā et misericordiā tu[
quā fecisti mecum ut saluares āia[
mēā · nec possum in monte saluari · n[
forte app̄hendat me malū et moria[
Est ciuitas hic iuxta · ad quā possu[
fugere parua · z saluabor in ea. Nūq[
nou modica est · et uiuet anima me[
Dixitq; ad eū . Ecce etiā in hoc suscep[
p̄ces tuas · ut nō subuertā urbem pr[
qua locutus es. Festing z saluare ibi[
quia nō potero facere quicq̄ donec i[
predaris illuc. Idcirco uocatum e[

Rookledge's International
**handbook of type designers:
a biographical directory**

Rookledge's
International **handbook of**

desi

a biographical directory

edited by
&

Sarema Press

type
ners:

by **Ron Eason**
& Sarah Rookledge,
Phil Baines
Gordon Rookledge

(Publishers) Ltd., 1991

First Edition 1991
Copyright © 1991 Gordon Rookledge
Published and distributed in the UK by
Sarema Press (Publishers) Ltd.
15 Beeches Walk, Carshalton Beeches, Surrey, England. SM5 4JS
Tel. 081-770 1953, Fax. 081-770 1957

British Library Cataloguing-in-Publication Data
Eason, Ronald, 1933-
Rookledge's international handbook of type designers:
a biographical directory.
I. Title. II. Rookledge, Sarah, 1962-
686. 220922
ISBN 1 870758 099

    Designed by Phil Baines and typeset in Swift (Gerard Unger)
and Bureau Grotesque 37 (FontBureau) using Quark XPress 3.0.
    Imagesetting by Manuscript Typesetting, Trowbridge, additional
typesetting by FMT Graphics Ltd., London.
    Printed & bound in Spain by Mateu Cromo.

    Endpapers: Gutenberg, Fust & Schoeffer, *42-Line Bible,* 1455,
(Photo: St.Bride Printing Library)

CONTENTS

PUBLISHER'S NOTE & ACKNOWLEDGMENTS

The original idea to put biographies of type designers in the first edition of *Rookledge's International Typefinder* in 1981 was not carried out due to cost and time constraints. When in 1989 Phil Baines was commissioned to revise the *typefinder,* he also suggested that some abridged biographies should be included. Subsequently when the writer, Sarah Rookledge (my daughter), was researching these she discovered there was no, single-volume reference book in existence. I therefore suggested a handbook of type designers' biographies should be published and this is the result.

I would like to thank the joint authors Ron Eason and Sarah Rookledge. Sarah, as a pioneer, had the difficult task of laying down the route and, like Phil, was instrumental with me in publishing this book, while Ron, who took over from Sarah, had the formidable task of stepping into some one else's shoes. Phil Baines, friend, editor, designer and 'emotional supporter' was an enormous help and did so much to keep the book going with his youthful energy, and dedication. All three have been a pleasure to work with.

While many people have given help, advice and encouragement during the two years this project has taken I would particularly like to thank the following: Nick Biddulph, René Kerfante of Monotype, the staff of St. Bride Printing Library, and all those companies and individuals who supplied such interesting material and information.

Gordon Rookledge, September 1991.

EDITORS' INTRODUCTION

This book is intended to bring together for the first time in a single-volume reference book, the lives and careers of over 175 men and women who have designed the majority of typefaces currently in use.

Biographies of type designers do exist—a few designers have had two or three; collections of shorter biographies have appeared, notably in D.B.Updike's *Printing Types,* Sebastian Carter's *Twentieth Century Type Designers,* and Lawrence W.Wallis's *Modern Encyclopedia of Typefaces 1960-90;* and individual biographies have appeared over the years in manufacturer's magazines such as the *Montotype Recorder* and the *Linotype Matrix*—but many of these are now out of print and only accessible in specialized libraries. This volume does not attempt much fresh research of a highly academic nature, rather it seeks to bring together in a convenient format, information from a range of sources and in so-doing to stimulate interest in type and in those who have made it their responsibility to design it.

The term type designer is open to several interpretations— for example: the person who prepares strict guidelines when commissioning a face; the drawer of a face; the punch-cutter; the person editing outlines on-screen—and in this book you will find designers who do each of these and a few who do all, but the only definition that seems to work is 'the person most responsible for the final appearance of a typeface'.

Although we have limited the book to designers of text typefaces, display typography does come into our story with the nineteenth-century designers and foundries, but generally we regard it as a separate study.

From 1455 to about 1930, we have tried to include every-
body that a general reader might ever expect to come across,
and for the sake of historical completeness have added a few
designers for whom no current typeface exists. From about
1930, the problem is more difficult—the sheer number of
typefaces issued and the speed of change—the major figures
are obviously here, and we have included designers from the
major manufacturers and some of the 'young lions' who are
changing the way we think about and look at type today. We
hope the book does not seem overburdened by twentieth century designers, rather that it reflects the way things are.

As far as available source material allows, we have tried to
reflect the various designers' importance and influence by
the length of their entry, but this is not always possibe. Little
is recorded about the lives of many type designers; partly due
to the relative anonymity of their profession , and partly due
to the time in which they lived. For many designers it is difficult to give firm dates and in at least one case, writers cannot
agree on his country of birth.

There will no doubt be some debate as to the merit (or lack
thereof) regarding some of our selection, particularly in the
modern section, and criticism of a constructive nature is wel-
comed in the event of there being a second edition.

Phil Baines & Gordon Rookledge,
London, September 1991

FOREWORD by Lawrence W.Wallis

Since the seminal invention of movable type by Gutenberg in the middle of the fifteenth century, the physical form of type has changed profoundly through several evolutionary steps.

Movable type was cast from molten metal in an adjustable hand mould from letter matrices struck from hand-engraved punches. Much of the skill resided with a punch-cutter whose interpretative powers determined in large measure the success or otherwise of the alphabet being produced. It was initially a handicraft process from beginning to end, but underwent mechanisation in the late nineteenth century with the advent of the pantographic punch-cutting machine and the mechanical composition systems such as Linotype and Monotype.

In the late 1940s, the next evolutionary development tentatively started to unfold with the installation of photocomposition systems where the typographic master fonts had transmogrified into photographic negatives in the shape of discs, grids, and filmstrips; a technology that quickly succumbed to digital phototypesetting which originated in the middle of the 1960s.

Digital fonts are somewhat abstract and not instantly recognisable as collections of alphabets, but occur as mathematical descriptions for storage in computer memory. Initially the character shapes were expressed as compressed bitmaps for exposure to photo-sensitive film or paper via generation on a cathode ray tube (CRT).

With the progression of time, the digital encoding of fonts became more refined with the outline shapes of characters expressed as vectors and later more satisfyingly as Bezier curves (in PostScript composition) or quadratic curves (in TrueType composition). Laser imaging is now the preferred method of output.

Throughout the succession of technological changes in typography over the 550 years from the middle of the fifteenth century, an ever-present constant has been that the design for an alphabet must commence as a conception of the human intellect and imagination and committed to paper as a working drawing. This book tells the story of many of the individuals who have contributed with originality to the creation, design, and drafting of typographic alphabets. At a time of intense technical upheaval, the need in a subject for some compass bearings, some reference points, or some benchmarks is of paramount importance in order to preserve and to perpetuate the best of traditions. The following pages contribute handsomely to that objective.

Anonymity is a characteristic very much associated with the exercise of type design, especially in alphabets intended for continuous reading which constitute the primary concern of this book. General readers are usually blissfully unaware of the nuances and subtleties contributing towards the character of a particular type design. This is especially true of good and effective book and related typography. If the best type fonts for run-on setting are anonymous, the designers behind them are even more so. It is a fate shared with many architects of fine buildings. Much of the shroud of anonymity is instructively removed from the designers featuring in the ensuing pages, as well as from some of the enterprises that commissioned alphabets from them.

Without doubt, *Rookledge's International handbook of type designers* has compressed a great deal of information into a convenient form for the student, enthusiast, designer, scholar, and layman with an interest in typography. It will rank alongside *Rookledge's International typefinder* as an essential work of reference and no better recommendation can be given.

L.W.W. 1991

hist-

orical introduction: an outline of the main trends in type design *by* Phil Baines

When Johann GUTENBERG perfected the art of printing in 1455 with his *42-Line Bible* he was answering the need of an ever-growing readership that the manuscript trade was unable to satisfy. It was the Renaissance, and within ten years, printing had reached Italy, the centre of that great explosion of learning, in another ten it was being practiced throughout most of Europe.

While the unique and essential features of his invention (*) were to remain virtually unchanged for the next 400 years, the typeface he used—a heavy black script called textura—was to last less than twenty.

Gutenberg's type was designed to look like the manuscripts it replaced, but it was dark and did not suit the spirit of the age. In Subiaco, Italy, SCHWEYNHEIM & PANNARTZ produced what is generally regarded as the first roman type in 1465.

Old face venetians

Italy became the centre for fine printing, in particular Venice. It was there in 1470 that Nicolas JENSON cut his famous type. The letters have an oblique, calligraphic stress; the change from thick to thin strokes is gradual whilst the serifs are strong and steeply sloped. The most obvious characteristic is the sloping cross-bar to the lower-case e, and types with these characteristics are generally referred to as old face venetians.

(*) **The essentials of Gutenberg's invention:** An adjustable hand-mould, with punch-stamped matrices for precision casting of type-sorts in large quantities; a type-metal alloy with a low melting point but rapid and undistorted solidification; and a press similar to those used by paper makers and book binders.

The style was virtually ignored after Jenson's time until the late-nineteenth century when William MORRIS, leader of the English Arts & Crafts movement, turned his attention to typography. Several notable revivals ensued, among them Morris's own Golden (1890), COBDEN-SANDERSON's Doves Press Roman (1891) and BRUCE ROGERS' Centaur (1915).

Old face

A generation after Jenson, the great Renaissance publisher and printer Aldus MANUTIUS published Cardinal Bembo's *De Aetna* using a new set of types. Developed from the earlier venetians, they became the model for European type design for the next 250 years. Printers of each generation from Manutius to CASLON used this basic letter form with differences in emphasis only.

The design followed the underlying principles of Jenson's type and the most obvious difference is a straight cross-bar to the lower-case e, but Aldus' type had a better balanced set of capitals and lower-case, while the letter fit was more even. These factors and Aldus' position as a pioneer of cheap and accurate editions ensured their success. (†)

The design was further refined in France from 1540 onwards by Claude GARAMOND and later Jean JANNON and Robert GRANJON. French types were bought by Dutch printers such as Christopher PLANTIN and Cristoffel VAN DIJCK (who darkened the design a little), and their types were in turn bought by English printers, notably Dr. FELL of Cambridge. William Caslon I was the first English printer and typefounder to satisfy the home market, and his types (started in 1725), the last of the old face category, followed these Dutch models.

Transitional

Transitional faces first appeared in England and France in the mid-eighteenth century. The transition implied by the name was from the old-face types already mentioned, and the modern faces of DIDOT and BODONI with their vertical shad-

---

(†) A note about italics: The first italic typeface is usually accepted as that of Aldus Manutius, first used in 1501; mean and cramped it was designed to save space in pocket editions. Other earlier italics took as their models the cursive formal hand of the Italian writing masters such as ARRIGHI in Rome and Tagliente in Venice. Although only a lower-case matched with roman capitals, the italic was originally used as an independent face. Today it is regarded generally as an accompaniment to a roman and is little used alone.

ing and abrupt contrast between thick and thin strokes.

The first typefaces of the kind are generally accepted as being Pierre Simon FOURNIER's roman of 1750 and John BASKERVILLE's of 1757, although they were both preceded by GRANDJEAN's Romains du Roi of 1702. All three types mark a definite break with the past, with their more vertical stress and greater contrast between thick and thin strokes, they paved the way for the next development.

Modern

Baskerville's type and typography—his generous use of space and lack of ornament—was frowned upon in Britain during his lifetime but was highly influential on the continent. While in Britain, William MARTIN and Richard AUSTIN were content to condense the basic letterform and sharpen the serifs, continental designers took the trend further and created the so-called modern face. Firmin Didot, c.1784, Giovanni Battista Bodoni in 1798 and Justus Eric WALBAUM, c.1800, imposed a strict vertical stress and changed the thin strokes and serifs into hair-lines. These types demanded exacting presswork and high quality paper to achieve the desired, dazzling effect. The resultant types were 'designed' rather than 'drawn' and the abrupt vertical stress makes them difficult to read in any quantity without the use of generous leading.

Up to, and including the appearance of the modern letter, just described, typeface design was a continual process of refinement but during the nineteenth century industrialisation altered peoples' perceptions of print and a much more fragmented development took place as new kinds of letterforms appeared—initially in England—to join the roman and italic.

Egyptians

The first of these new forms is now known as egyptian after Vincent FIGGINS' typeface of that name issued in 1817. Quickly followed by other founders, egyptians have been described as the 'first original design of advertising type'. With their heavy, even weight and matching slab-serifs they were designed for impact and aggression not legibility or sensitivity. More refined twentieth-century versions of the basic letterform are Rockwell (1934), Adrian FRUTIGER's Serifa (1967) and Margaret CALVERT's, Calvert (1980).

Clarendons & ionics

A letterform similar in general proportions to the egyptians but with strongly bracketed serifs is clarendon, which takes its name from from the first version of this style cut by Benjamin Fox in 1845. Originally, clarendons were slightly condensed letters and were designed as a bold-face to accompany the modern roman then in use. Subsequently expanded versions appeared and later still, additional weights. Clarendons are characterised by a large x-height (for legibility), a strong horizontal emphasis and an almost architectural sturdiness. With some refinement to the weight, they are ideal for printing on poor quality paper such as newsprint. Many newspaper types follow this pattern and are often referred to as ionics after C.H.GRIFFITHS' typeface of that name which was issued in 1922.

Sans serif, sometimes called grotesque

At the same time as the egyptians and clarendons, sans serifs appeared. The first was Caslon's so-called Egyptian of 1816—a clumsy unbalanced set of capitals probably intended for headings and emphasis only—but it was the German founders who developed the style in the 1830's.

While British sans serifs of the nineteenth century tended to be heavy, with capitals of even width and modern-face features to G ,R, g and t, the German types reformed the style, the capitals differ in width while the stokes taper; BERTHOLD's Akzidenz Grotesk of 1898 is typical of this approach. American sans serifs tended to draw on both sources, often using British forms but German stroke treatment as typified by M.F.BENTON's News Gothic of 1908.

During the first half of this century the development of the sans serif took two distinct routes. In Britain in 1916 London Underground began using a sans serif typeface designed for them by Edward JOHNSTON, based on classical Roman proportions it was a break with previous sans serifs. This same approach was adopted and refined in Gill Sans by his friend and pupil Eric GILL in 1928. In Germany, designs were influenced by Bauhaus ideas of purity of form and developed along geometric lines. Paul RENNER's Futura, (1928) is the most popular of this kind and has been widely copied.

After World War II, the idea of a sans serif typeface with an extended family of related weights arose on the continent, especially in Switzerland where Bauhaus principles had been diluted to resemble abstract pattern making. Adrian Frutiger's Univers series, begun in 1952, was the first and most ambitious of these, with twenty-eight weights all mathematically related and worked out from the outset. Its popularity, however, was eclipsed by Max MEIDINGER's Helvetica of

1957. Based on Akzidenz Grotesk, its large family of weights has been added haphazardly over the years.

More recent sans serifs have concentrated on introducing a little more humanity and do not fit easily into any of the above categories. Notable examples are Frutiger (1977) and Otl AICHER's Rotis of 1988.

Twentieth-century romans

While all these other letterforms were appearing, the roman letter continued to slowly evolve. For much of the nineteenth century, the modern letter was used for the bulk of text setting. But it was a debased version of the elegant Didot's & Bodoni's, coupled with poor setting and indifferent presswork, that led to William Morris's typographic revolution in the 1890's and the revival of interest in old face venetians as already noted.

In the early years of the twentieth century it was mainly the manufacturers of foundry type who instigated new type design while manufactures of the newly-introduced mechanical composition machines spent much of their efforts on reviving the 'classic faces' of previous centuries. By the 1930's all these 'classic faces' had been revived, cut in facsimile, or had a type 'cut in the spirit of'. However, mechanical composition and changes in printing—higher speeds, smoother papers—soon led to new designs. MASON's Imprint (1912), PIERPONT's Plantin (1913) and MORISON's Times New Roman (1933), while relying on old face forms, showed that the new century needed its own types.

Aside from the revivals and those based loosely on previous models, categorising twentieth century romans is not possible in the same sense as those of previous centuries, where appearance and age are one and the same. Many allude to more than one historical period—Matthew CARTER's Bitstream Charter has the feel of an ionic but the serifs and stress of and old-face; some draw their influence on sources outside lettering—Eric Gill's inscriptional-based Perpetua—and many are just themselves: Gerard UNGER's Demos or Zuzana LICKO's Matrix, results of their designers' time, place and technology.

The influence of technology: the pantograph & mechanical composition, photo/film/CRT/laser setting, the Macintosh

The explosion of new kinds of letterforms—and all the decorated faces not discussed here—was very much a result of industrialisation. During the last 100 years or so there have been three major technological developments which have changed the practice of type design.

The first was the pantograph punch-cutting machine invented by L.B.BENTON in 1884, the first significant departure from Gutenberg's invention of over 400 years earlier.

At last, type could be designed on a drawing board and translated directly into matrices without the technical and economic restrictions of engraving a punch in metal at its actual size.

The second development, allied to the growth of offset-litho printing, was the development of photo-setting after World War II. The matrix for the type was no longer a brass die but a photographic negative. Without the economic constraints of metal type production, typeface production was neither costly in terms of time nor in terms of capital outlay. Although still used to describe all 'post-metal' typesetting, photosetting is now a misnomer; type is now generally stored as mathematical formulæ in digital form, (a technique first introduced by the German firm of Hell in 1965), and is output to either bromide paper or film via a Cathod Ray Tube (CRT) or laser output device.

The third development is strictly a progression from the photo/digital technology but because of its impact can, I think, be considered separately, and that is the Apple Macintosh computer. Introduced in 1984 as a low-cost personal computer with a user-friendly-interface, the 'Mac' has developed into a comprehensive graphic, design and typesetting tool because of its immediacy and flexibility. Using digital types in PostScript format, (now supplied by all manufacturers) the 'Mac' has taken typesetting away from typesetters and put it in the hands of designers (and everyone else), thus de-mystifying the whole production process. More recently, with the arrival of type-designing programs such as FontStudio, everyone has the opportunity to design type themselves. The result of this new democracy is most visible in the works of Neville BRODY and Zuzana LICKO whose work has started to change perceptions and challenge accepted notions of beauty and legibility.

These are exciting times.

a biog-

raphical directory:
[Adobe Systems Inc. *to* Gudrun Zapf-von Hesse]
by Ron Eason
& Sarah Rookledge

KEY

Countries of designers' birth are shown using the standard international motoring abbreviations.

Typefaces are listed chronologically. Generally, the date is the release date of the face, which may differ by many years from the design date. Typeface dates are a problem area, as sources do not always agree, and even manufacturers' dates can be innaccurate. Typefaces for which we have found no dates are listed last.

Typefaces in italics are revivals.

[Typefaces within brackets] are named after a particular designer but are not designed by them.

Numbers in bold are references to typeface samples in *Rookledge's international typefinder,* 2nd edition, 1990.

NAMES IN SMALL CAPS indicate other biographies in this handbook.

ADOBE Systems Inc.   USA

Adobe Systems in California, USA, are the developers of
PostScript, the computer page description language that
enables type and graphic images to be combined in one doc-
ument. Introduced in 1983, PostScript is the most common
digital font format used for electronic publishing on Macintosh, IBM and NeXt computers. It encodes type designs as outlines made up of bezier curves and is device-independent. It
will work on any device possessing a PostScript interpreter,
from the 72dpi resolution of a standard Mac screen to the
1200lpi and more, of a photographic imagesetter.

All the major type suppliers now produce type in this format, it no longer has to be output on their own machines and
can be combined with type from another manufacturers.

Adobe operates a type library of over 600 PostScript fonts,
consisting of original and licensed faces and, in addition,
develops and markets a range of software tools for graphic
designers.

The director of typography since 1984 has been the type
designer Sumner STONE.

RCE

AGFA COMPUGRAPHIC,
see COMPUGRAPHIC

Otl AICHER   b.1922   D

Rotis Family: serif, semi-serif, semi-sans, sans (1988)
Traffic

A designer with a worldwide reputation in the field of corporate identity, Otl Aicher has also made a major contribution to type design and typography, not least through his writing.

He was born at Ulm in Germany and after World War II studied sculpture at Munich Academy of Fine Arts. At the Hochschule für Gestaltung in Ulm, of which he was a founder, he headed the development group, lectured on visual communications and was for a time its principal.

He designed the typeface Traffic which is used in the public transport systems in Munich and at Munich Airport, but his best known design is the typeface family Rotis, in which he has tried to combine elements of both serif and sans serif in his search for ultimate legibility.

He has written books on design theory including *Typographie* (1988). One proposition advanced in his writing is that art and typography are irreconcilable: one is concerned with conveying information the other with appearance.

RCE

AMERICAN TYPEFOUNDERS' now Kingsley ATF
USA

The American Typefounders' Company was formed in 1892 from 23 of the 30 or so type foundries operating throughout America at that time. It was really a case of economic necessity, because although the demand for type was greater than ever before there were too many foundries, with the result that competition was fierce and profit margins had all but disappeared. The solution was to form a 'trust' and reduce the number of centres where type was cast and thus reduce operating costs and restore stability to the industry.

Printers were apprehensive about the move and some typefounders chose to remain independent and advertised themselves as 'not in the trust'. But on the whole the idea was a sensible one because even more radical changes were in store for the industry with the invention of automatic typecasting.

Newspaper production had already moved towards automatic typecasting with the LINOTYPE hot-metal, line-casting machine which was first installed at the New York Tribune in

1886, and by the early years of the twentiethth century Monotype, Compositype, Thompson and others were producing devices that enabled printers to produce their own type. ATF tackled this challenge by producing the best possible type with a reputation for hardness, uniformity, print alignment, depth of drive and finish. It also adopted a policy of originating its own type designs, which were generally more adventurous than those of the large machinery manufactures at that time, and negotiated royalty agreements on other type designs.

Among the type designers who worked for ATF at that time were Joseph W.PHINNEY who had been with the Dickinson foundry in Boston and who persuaded Robert W Nelson to buy into the company. Nelson soon became general manager and made a significant contribution to the prosperity of the company and later became its president. Another important figure at ATF was its chief technical advisor, Linn Boyd BENTON, inventor of the automatic punch-cutting machine, who set up the type design department, the first of its kind in any foundry. Later, Benton's son, Morris Fuller Benton, joined his father at ATF and became one of the most prolific type designers of all time with over 200 typefaces to his credit including eighteen versions of Century.

In 1926 Robert Nelson died and the company's fortunes declined and eventually it went into voluntary bankruptcy. But by 1936, under the presidency of Thomas Roy Jones, the company had revived again and two years later it entered the offset lithography field with the purchase of Webendorfer-Wills Company. During the 1960s ATF became a subsidiary of Whitin Machine Works but in 1966 Whitin and ATF were acquired by White Consolidated Industries, the descendent of White Sewing Machine Company. In 1970 ATF acquired Lanston Monotype. More recently as a result of further mergers the company became known as Kingsley ATF.

In addition to typeface design, they now manufacture software packages for use on Macintosh computers including ATF TypeDesigner, which allows the production of PostScript, TrueType, NeXt and IBM compatible fonts and an optical scaling programme, the first of its kind, which goes some way towards compensating for the inherent defects of having a single drawing for each typeface.

RCE

Ludovico degli ARRIGHI, da Vincenza   d.1527 I
& Antonio BLADO   active 1515-67 I

Arrighi/Centaur Italic (1925, see Frederic WARDE)
Blado italic **380**

Antonio Blado is the best known of the Italian printers who, in the fifteenth and sixteenth centuries, began to replace the scribes who had previously worked on the mass of documents issued by the Papal Chancery in Rome. Among the types he used was the 1527 italic of Ludovico degli Arrighi.

Ludovico degli Arrighi was a professional calligrapher and later a printer of fine editions who also designed type. He was the first calligrapher to print specimens of his scripts, which he did in *La Operina* (1522) and *Il modo de temperare le penne* (1523). *La Operina* was printed from wood blocks but the later book uses his first italic type, the earliest formal chancery italic. In 1524 he started a small press with Lautitius Perugino, a printer but also an engraver and as such probably the cutter of Arrighi's types.

They printed fine editions of short contemporary works using type based on Arrighi's formal cursive script. Arrighi used another version of this type for books published in 1526 and 1527 after Lautitius had left the company, and it was a font of this later type which the printer Antonio Blado acquired and used for many publications, the first of which was Sannazaro's *Sonetti* in 1530. Blado was the printer to Pope Paul III and also printer of, among other works, Machiavelli's first editions.

Stanley MORISON supervised an adaptation of the type as it appears in Blado's *Nuova Poesia Toscana* of 1539. Named Blado it accompanies Poliphilus, the 1923 facsimile of the 1499 roman of Aldus MANUTIUS. The other type based on the Arrighi italic and named Arrighi, was designed by Frederic Warde for MONOTYPE in 1925. Cut by Charles Plumet it accompanies Bruce ROGERS' Centaur. A LINOTYPE version of this is known as Vincenzia

Nothing is known of Arrighi after 1527 and it has been suggested that he died in the sack of Rome, but his types and his own severe unornamented style of book design had influenced many of his contemporaries.

SR

Arrighi's second italic of 1526 used in *Vita Sfortiæ clariss. ducis...*
printed by Antonio Blado in 1539.   (Photo: St. Bride Printing Library)

Decurionum, & equitum in uinculis retento. Braccius
enim in Vmbria felici rerum successu elatus, uasta cupidi-
tate animum intenderat, ut urbis Romæ imperio potiretur.
Tribus siquidem ea tempestate Pontificibus, immani Cardi
nalium ambitione, atque superbia creatis, christiana religio
lacerabatur : Roma que terrarum quondam Domina, fame,
pestilentia, ac incendijs deformata, obsessa latronibus, ac or-
bata Pontifice, factiosorum libidini seruiebat. Ad id auden
dum, patrandumque facinus , idoneus, & opportunus erat
Tartalia : quum sub signis eius mille equites, & bis toti-
dem pedites militarent. Fœdere itaque icto, ut mutuis auxi
lijs, atque opibus fines proferrent, & sese aduersus uim ho-
stium tuerentur, Tartalia facile cuncta usque ad Senensium
fines in potestatem redegit, præter Aquenses, & Porsenia
nos, qui Sfortianorum præsidio tenebantur. Braccius uero po
sitis ad Anienem castris, fusisq; tumultuario prælio Roma-
norum copijs urbe potitus est. Per eos quoque dies Braccius Michaletum, qui, capto Sfortia, ad eum amicitiæ iure cum
trecentis equitibus confugerat, omni pudore dissoluto mis-
sum fecit, nec persoluto quidem stipendio. Quam demum
contumeliam indignatus Braccio Picininus, magno, nobiliq;
animo resarciuit, quum ex domestico abaco argentum omne,
ut æs alienum cum milite dissolueretur, ad Michaletum detu
lisset. Per hunc modum inter se diducti, accensiq; odio Sfor
tia, & Braccius Italicæ militiæ principes effecti, magnosq;

Charles Robert ASHBEE 1863-1942 GB

Endeavour
Prayer Book

Architect, designer and social reformer, Charles Robert Ashbee was a major force behind the Arts & Crafts Movement which glorified the ideals of mediæval craftsmanship.

Born at Isleworth on the western outskirts of London, he was the only son of a highly successful businessman who is today duly acknowledged as the foremost collector and bibliographer of erotica in Victorian Britain.

In 1888, after Cambridge and two years in an architect's office, Ashbee founded the Guild of Handicrafts, and its attendant school, for which headquarters were set up at Essex House in the Mile End Road in the East End of London, a predominantly working-class area. After the death of William MORRIS in 1896, he took over the plant and equipment of the Kelmscott Press to found the Essex House Press. Book production became the most important activity at Essex House and it was not long before Ashbee began designing type.

His first effort was a set of decorated initials produced in 1899. This was followed by Endeavour, a type very much on the lines of Morris's Golden Type, and later by Prayer Book, a type specially created for a luxurious, limited edition of the *Prayer Book* produced by the Essex House Press to commemorate the accession of Edward VII in 1902. Ashbee's types are highly idiosyncratic and combine archaic elements such as ligatures with art nouveau influences such as barbed serifs and exaggerated descenders.

The Essex House Press was small but influential, a distinction which it shared with a number of similar private presses which operated in England at the turn of the century; however, its influence was never as great as that of the Kelmscott Press of William Morris, or the Doves Press operated by COBDEN- SANDERSON and Emery WALKER

RCE

George AURIOL 1863-1938 F

Auriol (1901-4)
La Français
L'Auriol
Champleve
Le Clair de Lune
Le Robur

George Auriol (born Jean Georges Huyot) was a French graphic artist whose work exemplifies the art nouveau style practiced in Paris in the late nineteenth and early twentieth centuries.

When he was twenty, Auriol, an occasional contributor to literary reviews, had a piece accepted by *The Black Cat*, the journal of the Black Cat Cabaret in Paris. This magazine was founded in 1882 and ran for ten years. At the end of 1883 Auriol joined the staff. He knew many of the artists who attended the cabaret including Van Gogh and Toulous-Lautrec (for whom he designed a rubber stamp), and Eugene Grasset, who designed the typeface Grasset for PEIGNOT & Sons at the instigation of Georges Peignot. In 1900 Georges Peignot asked Auriol to do the same. The result was the typeface Auriol. A version of this face appeared in 1900 in *Chansons d'Atelier* by Paul Delmet but the type was subsequently modified to give it its present form. Auriol, with it's distinctive 'M', was the basis for the lettering used by Hector Guimard for the entrance signs to the Paris Metro. It was re-released by Deberny & Peinot in 1979 with a new bold.

Other typefaces followed quickly as did a series of typographic ornaments but the time which Auriol spent as a type designer was short, less than three years. Two books on typography written and designed by François Thibaudeau and published in 1921 and 1924 were set in a combination of Auriol's typefaces and also used his ornaments. When Peignot & Sons became Deberny & Peignot and moved into new premises, Auriol designed the decorations on the front of their new factory.

SR

George Auriol: lettering from *The sign painter's letter book*, 1906.
(Photo: St. Bride Printing Library)

**Richard AUSTIN,
see BELL**

Colin BANKS   b.1932   GB
& John MILES   b.1931   GB

Post Office Double Line (1973)
New Johnston (1980)
Phonebook (1984-87)

The partnership of Banks & Miles is best known for designing a number of corporate identities for British public insti-
tutions and the typefaces listed above all form part of such a
project.

The two men met as students on a City & Guilds Design
Course in Kent, worked separately for a while (John Miles with
Jan VAN KRIMPEN and Sem HARTZ at ENSCHEDÉ in Holland),
then went into partnership in 1958.

Their New Johnston typeface was designed for London
Transport and is an updating of the original type designed by
Edward JOHNSTON in 1916. Johnston designed a medium only,
a bold being added later by William Pickering. The lack of display sizes meant that by the late 1970s London Transport pub-
licity material appeared in an assortment of typefaces and
the corporation were considering adopting Helvetica instead
to reintroduce some stylistic consistency. Banks & Miles,
appointed to create a new identity for London Transport, persuaded them to keep Johnston but modified the face,
increased the range of sizes and adapted it for photosetting.

New Johnston is a heavier type with altered stroke endings
and a larger x height than the original. It first appeared in
1980 and has subsequently been converted to PostScript format for use on Macintosh computers.

Banks & Miles have also revised four faces: Excelsior for
MONOTYPE, Plantin and Garamond for Bopst, and Plantin for
Purdy MacIntosh. In addition to this they have produced a
number of proprietary typefaces.

SR

John BASKERVILLE   1706-75   GB

Baskerville (1924) **77-80**

John Baskerville's contribution to printing is enormous. He
adapted the old face roman to produce highly influential new

types; he recognised the important role of typography in book design; he modified inks and the printing press to give blacker, sharper letters on the page and was responsible for the introduction of wove paper. Baskerville's work influenced continental printers like DIDOT and BODONI, but in his native England it was frequently derided.

Like William CASLON, John Baskerville was born in Worcestershire but in 1725 he moved to Birmingham where he worked as a writing-master and cut inscriptions on gravestones. The *Baskerville Slate,* now in the Birmingham City Library is a sample to show the styles of letter he could cut. Later when he was to design his own types he could draw on the knowledge of lettering acquired in this period. He taught writing for ten years, then decided to take advantage of the fashion for japanware—japanning is a method of decorating, giving porcelain a glossy finish—and his business prospered making him a prominent figure in Birmingham society.

When it came to making money out of printing Baskerville's perfectionism worked against him. Fortunately he had a substantial income from another business on which he could draw.

In 1750, aged 44, he set up a printing press but the pace of his work and the exacting standards he set himself were such that it was to take him seven years to produce his first book. Existing types, inks and presses did not meet his standards and despite lacking any printing background he determined to improve all of them. The type was cut for him by John Handy (d.1792) who, by the time of Baskerville's death, had worked for him for at least 28 years. By 1752 he had cut fourteen letters, a year later he had enough type to produce an advertisement for Baskerville's first book, an edition of *Virgil* which finally appeared in 1757.

It is now regarded as a landmark in the history of typography, and like all his books—and unlike those of most of his contemporaries—it did not depend on illustrations for its effect but relied on good types cleanly printed, with a judicious use of leading and letter spacing. He altered his presses to print with less impression, used a much blacker ink than his contemporaries and finally, he passed the printed sheets through a succession of hot copper cylinders to give the printed page a crispness and contrast not previously seen. At the time however, the type was much criticised and compared unfavourably to Caslon's. People said it was difficult to read, even that it would damage the sight, but it also had its

John Baskerville, portrait by Millar.   (Photo: F.E.Pardoe)

advocates, notably Benjamin Franklin. Baskerville described his aims in the preface to Milton's *Paradise Lost*, published in 1758:

> Having been an early admirer of the beauty of Letters, I became insensibly desirous of contributing to the perfection of them. I formed to myself ideas of greater accuracy than have yet appeared, and have endevoured to produce a *Sett of Types* according to what I perceived to be their true proportion.

In that same year, Baskerville acheived one of his ambitions as a printer: permission to print the Bible for the Cambridge University Press. Published on 4 July 1763, it bought him great acclaim on the continent and is regarded by many as his finest work. Unfortunately he couldn't sell enough copies to cover his costs, got discouraged, and temporarily withdrew from printing. The press was taken over by his fore-man Robert Martin (brother of William MARTIN who cut types for BULMER at the Shakespeare Press). Robert Martin brought in money through the sale of types but eventually Baskerville objected to his taking on printing for a rival firm and re-sumed control.

After Baskerville died in 1775, Robert Martin continued to print for a time using his master's types, but his work was only typical of the worst printing of the period. Baskerville's widow sold the remaining stock to Pierre-Augustin Caron de Beaumarchais for 150,000 francs for an edition of the works of Voltaire.

Although Baskerville's type influenced the work of Isaac MOORE and William Martin, most English printers persisted in their use of the old face, Caslon, and his type was largely forgotten during the nineteenth century. They were 'redis-covered' in 1917 by Bruce ROGERS and several revivals fol-lowed. The MONOTYPE version of 1924 is based on the Great Primer size used in the *Terence* of 1772, a LINOTYPE version appeared in 1931, and one by DEBERNY & PEIGNOT who made new matrices from the original punches. In 1953 the compa-ny presented these punches to Cambridge University.

Baskerville was buried standing-up in an adapted wind-mill in the grounds of his home at Easy Hill, near Birming-ham. Reflections on the truth or otherwise of the Book of Revelation which he made in his will led to his being brand-ed an atheist and when the windmill had to be demolished there were problems in finding a new home for the body. The corpse's unfortunate career included a period behind the counter of a plumber's, where it was exhibited for a fee, and the coffin didn't find a final resting place until well over a hundred years after his death.

SR

Johann Christian BAUER   active 1837-67   D

Roman Extra Bold (1850, modified 1957)
Verdi (1951)

& Bauersche Giesserei

At the beginning of the nineteenth century Great Britain was acknowledged throughout the world as the centre where the art of punch-cutting and typefounding had reached its high-est attainment. Consequently, when Johann Christian Bauer started the Bauer foundry at Frankfurt am Main in 1837 it was to Great Britain that he came to learn and perfect his skill in these arts.

Johann Christian Bauer was a craftsman of the old order who exemplified the spirit of the new industrial age. A skilful mechanic and a trained locksmith, his aim and ideal was to be able to carry out every task in the foundry with his own hands. With this purpose he came to Edinburgh in 1839 and worked for the firm of P.A.WILSON where he applied himself to learn the art of punch-cutting and eventually he formed his own concern under the name of Bauer, Furgusson & Huie.

Returning to Germany in 1847 he renamed his Company Englische Schriftschneiderei und Gravieranstalt (English Typecutting & Engraving Works). Although by nature a crafts-man rather than an industrialist (it is said that in his lifetime he cut more than 10,000 punches with his own hands) he turned his business into a worldwide concern in 20 years before his death in 1867.

Within six years of his death the foundry was sold to Eduard Kramer and August Schorr, and in 1880 Gustav Fuchs took the place of the latter. Fuchs turned the attention of the company to automatic typecasting and purchased the patent on the Komplett Typecasting Machine from Johnson & Atkinson. At the same time, John Mair Hepburn, who had worked on the development of this typecasting system for 25 years, was engaged as chief of the Mechanical Engineering Depart-ment of the company, now called Bauersche Giesserei. After some years of further development it was launched as the Universal Komplett Typecasting Machine and was considered a significant advance in mechanical typecasting.

By the turn of the century the emphasis was on mechani-cal composition rather than typecasting, and having already lost the newspaper trade to the newer foundries the company was in grave danger of losing the all-important book trade as well. However, in 1898 the company was bought by George Hartmann, the son of an old Frankfurt family, who soon realised that the competitive threat of mechanical composi-tion could only be met by raising the artistic standards of the foundry above those of its rivals by creating new and exiting typefaces.

George Hartmann had a flair for commissioning artists and designers, and during the 30 years of his leadership many distinguished artists, not necessarily type designers or typog-raphers, were encouraged to work in this field. Indeed, this was a departure which was almost unique to Germany at this time and may have been motivated by the fact that typography in Germany was still dominated by the black-letter with its mediæval overtones.

Whatever the reason, the result was that Germany, and in particular Bauersche Giesserei, became associated with a whole new movement in type design—Lucian BERNHARD, Paul RENNER, Heinrich JOST, Emil Rudolf WEISS, Imre REINER—artists such as these helped the company to conquer markets in Germany and also markets throughout the world, especially when the New York office was opened in 1927. Today the only remaining branch of the Bauer Foundry is in Barcelona, Spain where it operates under the name of Fundición Tipografica Neufville, SA.

RCE

Konrad F.BAUER 1903-70 D
& Walter BAUM D

Horizon/Imprimatur (1925) **389**
Alpha & Beta (1954)
Fortune/Volta (1955-56) **213**
Folio/Caravelle (1957-62) **275, 488**
Impressum (1962) **137**

Although no relation, Dr. Konrad F. Bauer was head of the art department at the Bauer Foundry in Frankfurt from 1928 until his retirement in 1968. He designed a number of typefaces, all with Walter Baum,they include Folio, a sans serif family based on nineteenth-century German models and Fortune the first clarendon to have a companion italic.
Konrad Bauer came from a printing family: his father had worked in two type foundries in Altona. He studied the history of art specialising in the history of lettering and he learnt calligraphy, before serving a printer's apprenticeship.

Dr Bauer was interested in the history of printing and wrote several books, pamphlets and articles including an article on the history of the Bauer foundry which appeared in Britain in *Typography* (Spring 1938).

In 1962 he instigated the revival of a competition for the most beautiful German book and headed the judging panel for thirteen years. He officially retired from the typefoundry in 1968 although in practice he continued to work for them until his death two years later.

SR

**Walter BAUM,
see BAUER (K.F.)**

Herbert BAYER   1900-85   A

proposal for a Universal type (1925)
Bayer Type (1933)

Through his work at the Dessau Bauhaus as head of the work-shop of Graphic Design & Printing from 1925 to 1928 and his later, more illustrative, work in the USA, Herbert Bayer was one of the most influential figures in twentieth-century graphic design.

An Austrian by birth, he arrived at the Bauhaus, then at Wiemar, in 1921 as a student, having worked in an architects office for two years. As a student his work was heavily influenced by Moholy Nagy and De Stijl and included the one- two- and three-million mark banknotes for the Bank of Thuringia in 1923. As a teacher he transformed the Bauhaus: out went lithographs and wood-cuts, in came moveable type and mechanical presses; out went serifs, black-letter and cap-ital letters, in came sans serif lower-case: asymmetric, simple and direct. What is thought of as 'Bauhaus typography' comes from these years.

Both his typeface designs reflect these beliefs and a strict adherence to geometric principles; they are rigorous in its application and stark in appearance. While neither make an effective text type, thy are part of an experiment which has occurred at intervals this century: Kurt SCHWITTERS, Brad-bury THOMPSON and Wim CROUWEL have also proposed single alphabet types of various kinds.

Bayer left the Bauhaus in 1928 and moved to Berlin, and in 1938, like many artists and designers in Germany, he fled the Nazi's and went to the USA. His work there was less dogmat-ic: he used photography, illustration and montage, with type playing a secondary role. He became an inspiration for post-war American designers and remained there till his death in Montecito, California in 1985.

PB

Peter BEHRENS   1868-1940   D

Behrens Roman (1902)

Like Otto Eckmann (1865-1900), Peter Behrens was influenced by the Arts & Crafts Movement, but purged of its mediæval-ism. He played a pivotal role in the transition from nine-teenth century decorative art to the simple, functional and geometric forms of the first half of the twentiethh century.

A native of Hamburg, he was educated at the Fine Arts School there before moving to Darmstadt and three years later became Director of the Dusseldorf School of Art.

The turning point in his career came in 1907 when Emil Rathenau the General Director of Allgemeine Elektricitäts-Gesellschaft (AEG) asked him to take charge of all areas of the company's visual identity including architecture, industrial design and graphic design. His work for AEG was the first example of a coordinated corporate identity.

For a period Walter Gropius was his assistant and it is like-ly that through him Behrens had an influence on the Bauhaus movement.

RCE

John BELL   1746-1831   GB
& Richard AUSTIN   GB

Fry's Ornamented (1796, re-issued 1949) **540**
Scotch Roman/Scotch No.2 (1907/20) **185/186**
Monotype Bell (1931) **172**

John Bell involved himself in virtually every aspect of the pro-duction and distribution of the printed word at a time when the professions with which he involved himself were becom-ing increasingly specialised and self-contained. He founded periodicals and newspapers, one of which, *The Morning Post* was published from 1772 until 1937. The pioneering typo-graphical style he used on *The World* was immediately copied by *The Universal Register* later to become *The Times*. With works like his 109-volume British Poets series he pioneered cheap editions of the classics, and he also furthered his aim of pop-ularising education when he took over the first London lend-ing library, The British Library, from its founder George Bathoe.

In 1788, inspired by Fournier's types, Bell started The British Letter Foundry and issued his first type specimen, cut by Richard Austin. A skilful cutter, Austin produced a very sharp letter which Stanley MORISON (who made a study of Bell's work) called the first English modern face. Actually the type retains some old style characteristics and should more properly be called a late transitional. Austin went on to cut true moderns and in 1819, when he had started a foundry of his own, he outlined the dangers of such designs being taken to extremes.

The British Letter foundry closed in 1798 and between this date and Austin's setting up The Imperial Letter Foundry in Worship Street, London, he cut types for the Wilson Foundry in Glasgow and for William Miller in Edinburgh. The MILLER & RICHARD types known as the Scotch Romans are probably his work. Austin also worked as a cutter of typographical ornaments and cut at least one decorated face: Fry's Ornamented.

The types Austin cut for Bell fell out of favour in Britain, though a small amount of Bell type remained at Cambridge, and, its origins forgotten, it acquired the name Georgian. In 1867 type cast from the original matrices (in the possession of founders STEPHENSON & BLAKE) were taken to the United States where it was known as Brimmer. Later D.B.Updike who admired Brimmer had Mountjoye cast in the same way. It was after learning of the origins of these types that Stanley Morison began his study of Bell which was published by Cambridge University Press in 1930. He then supervised the cutting of the facsimile Monotype Bell which was prepared in collaboration with Stephenson Blake. It was issued in 1931, the centenary of Bell's death. It was a study of Bell's life that began Stanley Morison's interest in newspapers, and which led subsequently to the design of Times New Roman.

SR

Edward BENGUIAT b.1927 USA

Souvenir (1970) **30, 469, 471**
Korinna(with Victor Caruso, 1974) **224**
Tiffany (1974) **27, 442**
Bauhaus (with Victor Caruso, 1975) **510, 515**
Bookman (1975) **57**
Benguiat (1978) **28**
Benguiat Gothic (1979) **297**
Barcelona (1981)
Panache (1988)

An American type designer with over 500 typefaces to his

credit, Edward Benguiat was vice-president of International Typeface Corporation and worked with Herb LUBALIN on the influential *U&lc* magazine doing much to develop its style.

He trained at the Workshop School of Advertising Art and studied calligraphy under Arnold Bank and Paul Standard. After becoming Associate Director of *Esquire* magazine in 1953 he opened his own design studio. In 1962 he joined Photo-Lettering Inc. where he is now Typographic Design Director and editor of their promotional publication *Plinc.*

In addition to typeface design he has created logotypes for the *New York Times, Playboy, Reader's Digest, Sports Illustrated, Esquire, Photoplay,* and *Look.*

RCE

Linn Boyd BENTON   1844-1932   USA

Century (1895, with Theodore L.De Vinne)

& Morris Fuller Benton   1872-1948   USA

Cloister Old Style (c.1897)
Alternate Gothic (1903)
Franklin Gothic (1903) **276**
Bold Antique/Whitin Black (1904)
Bodoni (1907)
Clearface (1907) **24**
News Gothic (1908)
Hobo (1910) **593**
Garamond (with T M Cleland 1917)
Century Schoolbook (1924) **119**
Bulmer (1928) **58**
Chic (1928)
Modernique (1928)
Novel Gothic (1928)
Parisian (1928)
Broadway (1929) **484**
Louvaine (1929)
Bank Gothic (1930-33) **290**
Stymie (1931) **199**
Agency Gothic (1933)
Benton/Whitehall (1934)
Tower (1934)
Phenix (1935)

In their different ways, both Linn Boyd Benton and his son Morris Fuller Benton made an enormous contribution to the development of type design, so much so that it would be difficult to say which man was the more eminent in this field.

Born in Little Fall, New York, Linn Boyd Benton spent his childhood in Milwaukee and La Crosse and increasingly during that time he developed a fascination for machinery of any kind; so much so that his father had to make him ration his time to ensure that he devoted at least some of it to other things.

His career started as a 'printer's devil', rolling the forms in the style of the day, and in this humble capacity he soon put his mechanical inventiveness to work by developing a method of handling the sheets which shortened the time at press.

His next job was in a paper store and type foundry where, through a succession of changing circumstances and financial deals, Benton eventually became the senior partner in the firm which became known as Benton Waldo & Co.

Throughout his time with the company (it was eventually absorbed into AMERICAN TYPEFOUNDERS') his mechanical flair and inventiveness ran parallel with his design and punch-cutting skills. An early example was a system of self-spacing type which enabled a compositor to increase productivity by 25-30%, but his masterpiece was undoubtedly the Benton Automatic Punch-cutter. Employing a system involving a pantograph and wax, it was a device that was capable of reproducing exquisite minuteness of detail. But more than this, it was an invention which came in the nick of time for Mergenthaler LINOTYPE, who at that particular moment in their history faced failure, if not ruin, unless they could find an adequate method of providing matrices for their new automatic typesetting machine. Indeed, it has been suggested that without Benton's punch-cutter, Linotype setting would not have been possible.

In the meantime Benton had invented yet another punch-cutter for his earlier 'self-spacing type machine', and once again Mergenthaler were quick to see the advantage and wasted no time in forming a leasing agreement with Benton.

As a type designer he is undoubtedly overshadowed by his son Morris Fuller Benton, however, Linn Boyd was famed as a punch-cutter and among his many achievements was the cutting of Century for Theodore L.DE VINNE's *Century* magazine.

When Benton Waldo & Co was absorbed into ATF, Robert

Nelson, ATF's director, asked Linn Boyd Benton to set up a type design department, the first of its kind in a foundry, and it was here that Linn Boyd's son, Morris Fuller Benton, joined his father as his assistant.

Morris Fuller Benton is accredited with being the most prolific type designer in American history, with an output twice as great as that of Frederic GOUDY: although in fairness Goudy did not start his career until a later age. The fact that Benton's father worked at the foundry until an advanced age (retaining his clarity of his thought and expression, it is said) did in all probability place an added strain on the younger man, but seems not to have diminished his remarkable output. A factor in his relative anonymity was his position as an in-house designer, but it was a position that suited his retiring character: when pressed he'd put his successes down to 'Lady Luck'.

Benton has been credited with inventing the concept of the type family and although this is not the case he did do his best work expanding faces (including some of Goudy's) into families and adapting existing type styles for ATF. Between 1900 and 1928 he designed 18 variations on Century, including the popular Century Schoolbook. Morris Benton also worked closely with his contemporary at ATF Henry Lewis Bullen, collector of the company's famous library and mentor of type publicist and scholar Beatrice Warde.

RCE

David BERLOW   b.1955   USA
& Roger BLACK   USA

New Caledonia (1979, DB)
Grotesque 13, 15, 17, 37, 53 & 79 (1990)
Empire (1989/90)
Agency (1990)
Belucian (DB)
New Century Schoolbook (DB)

David Berlow was born and lives in Boston, MA. and obtained a Bachelor of Science in Art at the University of Wisconsin, Madison. His career as a type designer began in 1977 at Mergenthaler, Linotype, Stempel and Haas where he was involved in a number of major projects including revisions of DWIGGINS' Caledonia, many of the ITC faces released by Mergenthaler.

After leaving Linotype in 1982 he joined Bitstream Inc, a newly-formed independent digital type foundry, where he worked in the Type Design, Technical and Marketing Departments as a senior designer and director. In 1989, with Roger BLACK, he co-founded The Font Bureau, an independent design firm specializing in consulting and contracting custom typographic products, and supplying fonts in PostScript format.

The headings in this book are set in Grotesque 37, a revival of a nineteenth-century type similar to STEPHENSON BLAKE's Grot 9 of 1906.

RCE

Lucian BERNHARD   1885-1972   D

Bernhard Antiqua (1912)
Bernhard Cursive/Madonna (1925)
Lucian (1925)
Bernhard Hand Brush Script (1928)
Bernhard Fashion (1929)
Bernhard Gothic (1929-30) **251**
Bernhard Roman (1937)
Bernhard Tango (1934) **323**
Lilith (1930) **562**
Bernhard Imago

A graphic artist with an international reputation for innovative poster design, Lucian Bernhard achieved his effect by using few words, frequently only one, and simple images. In his minimal designs he tried to achieve a distillation of the message to its simplest elements. Self-taught, he became a major force in poster design, a medium which had much greater significance in the first half of the century than it does today.

Born in Stuttgart, and educated in Zürich, he became Professor of Fine Arts at the Royal Akademie in Berlin before adopting America as his home, a step which many other European artists and designers were to take in the years leading up to World War II, and in 1929 he started designing typefaces for AMERICAN TYPEFOUNDERS'. True to the design principles demonstrated in his poster work, his typefaces are often economical and rational. Typical of this side of the Bernhard style are Bernhard Gothic, a slight sans serif in a variety of weights with an accompanying italic in the two smaller sizes, and Bernhard Fashion, an exceptionally light, almost weightless, sans serif.

He also produced some notable brush scripts, including Bernhard Hand Brush Script, an exceptionally heavy informal script, and Bernhard Cursive.

RCE

H.BERTHOLD AG   D

In 1858 Hermann Berthold opened a workshop for the manufacture of brass rule which eventually became the largest factory of its kind in Germany. When, in 1878, the German typefounding industry wanted to establish and standardise a system of type measurement they turned, not unnaturally, to the Berthold factory and commissioned Hermann Bertold to design and manufacture standard typographical gauges for universal application in the measurement of type. In due course these Berthold type metres became the basis of the Didot System of type measurement and are still in use today.

When Hermann Berthold died his successors added typefounding to the firm's activities and during the latter years of the century several well-known German foundries were absorbed. In 1919 the company purchased the original WALBAUM foundry, which had been sold to the publisher and printer F.A.Brockhaus in 1836 and moved to Leipzig from its original home in Weimar after the death of Walbaum's only son. Berthold thus became the owners of the original Walbaum punches and matrices.

In the following years Berthold employed or commissioned a number of distinguished type designers including Herbert POST, Imre REINER and Günther Gerhard LANGE.

In the years following World War II Berthold was the leading company associated with the introduction of phototypesetting and in 1958, the hundredth anniversary of the foundation of the company, they introduced the first commercial phototypesetting system, 'Diatype', which was succeeded by 'Diatext' in 1975 and 'Berthold ads 3000' in 1977 (ads stands for akzidenz-dialog-system).

Now one of the world's largest typefounders and manufacturers of photosetting equipment, Berthold licensed 500 typefaces from its 'Exklusiv' range to ADOBE for production as PostScript format fonts. The typefounding section of Berthold is now part of the Swiss typefoundry HAAS.

RCE

Raffaello BERTIERI   1875–   I

Inkunabula (1911)
Paganini (1928) **181**
Rondine (1948, with A. Butti)

Raffaello Bertieri, was primarily a printer and publisher and through his publishing house, Bertieri & Vansetti, he played a leading role in the development of higher standards of print in Italy at the start of this century.

He was born in Florence and at the age of eleven left school (for the needs of the family) to become apprenticed to a small local printing office. After a short excursion into the dramatic arts, at which he was self-taught, he returned to printing and at the age of 27 became a technical editor at a printing and publishing house in Milan. It was here that he began to develop his ideas in publishing.

His first title was the journal *Risorgiamento Grafico (Renaissance of the Graphic Arts)* which he began in 1903 and which rapidly became Italy's most influential publication in this field. Originally the title was owned jointly with his employers but within two years Bertieri became the sole owner.

With a friend called Vansetti he started the printing and publishing house in Milan called Bertieri & Vansetti, which played a leading role in the development of higher standards of print in Italy at the beginning of the century and published many art books for leading French and German publishers.

Bertieri & Vansetti also published the works of *Gabriele D'Annunzio* and *L'Arte di G B Bodoni*. His typeface Inkunabula, released by Nebiolo, is a roman based on the work of a Venetian printer Erhard Ratdolt..

RCE

Charles BIGELOW   b.1945   USA

Lucida (1985)
Leviathan
Pellucida
Syntax Phonetic

Charles Bigelow is a partner in the design studio of Bigelow & Holmes and assistant professor of Digital Typography at Stanford University, Conn. in the Department of Computer Science & Art.

A native of Michigan, he developed an early interest in typography as a result of his experience as a writer and editor at Cranbrook School. At Reed College in Oregon, where he graduated, he studied typography with Lloyd Reynolds and later with Jack Stauffacher in San Francisco.

In collaboration with his partner, Kris HOLMES, he has designed a number of typefaces including Lucida, an extended family of serif, sans serif, Greek, scientific and linguistic alphabets designed for laser printing which have been adopted by the journal *Scientific American*. A specifically computer orientated face is Pellucida, a related font family used on computer screens and artificial intelligence workstations. In contrast, Leviathan is a set of titling initials designed for the hand-set, letterpress edition of Moby Dick produced by the Arion Press. In collaboration with Hans Meier he has also produced Syntax Phonetic, a phonetic, typographic design for native American languages. He has also written two volumes of poetry.

RCE

BITSTREAM Inc., see CARTER (M)

Antonio BLADO, see ARRIGHI

Joseph BLUMENTHAL   1897-1990   USA

Spiral/Emerson (1930, italic 1936)

Joseph Blumenthal was a printer, historian, and author, as well as the designer of the typeface Spiral/Emerson.

Although he never worked for any of the private presses, Blumenthal took a great interest in their work, particularly that of Meynell's Nonesuch Press. He admired the work of Bruce ROGERS and the master printer D.B.Updike. He worked for publishers B.W.Huebsch Inc. (as a sales representative), William E. Rudge at Mount Vernon (as a compositor) and then briefly for A.G.Hoffman at the Marchbank Press. Together, Hoffman and Blumenthal set up a press called Spiral. The company did jobbing work for museums and publishers but occasionally printed books, such as Robert Frost's poetry for Random House.

When the depression forced a temporary shut-down of Spiral he sold the stock and machinery and left his native America for Europe. It was during this period that he designed the typeface Spiral. This face was cut for him by Louis Hoell of the BAUER foundry in 1930 and later cut for MONOTYPE with the addition of an italic in 1936 when the name was changed to Emerson.

On his return from Europe Spiral reopened again using the new typeface and continued printing until 1971. From then until his death in 1990 Blumenthal wrote on type and organised exhibitions. *Typographic Years, a printer's journey through a half-century 1925-75*, was written in 1982.

SR

Giovanni Battista BODONI   1740-1813   I

Bodoni (1907 & 1926, see BENTON *&* JOST*)*

Bodoni was one of the first cutters of a modern face, that is, a typeface which has hairline serifs at right angles to the uprights, vertical stress and abrupt contrast between thick and thin strokes. He took French types, such as FOURNIER's and those of the DIDOT's as his model. Bodoni was, in his day, the best known printer in Europe.

Bodoni was born in Turin in the north of Italy in 1740, the son of a printer. At eighteen he became a compositor at the press of the Propaganda Fide in Rome and at 28 was made director of the press of the Duke of Parma.

His early types are based on those of Pierre Simon Fournier, whose work he admired, but he experimented with these letter forms to create his own. The roman letter he cut in 1798 is what we generally mean by a Bodoni. The contrast of light and shade in his types can produce a sparkling effect on the page. The books which he printed reveal a taste for large sizes of type, generous use of white space and few ornaments. In addition to his romans Bodoni also produced a great many script types.

Bodoni received 300 francs a year towards his work from Napoleon Bonaparte and a further 18,000 francs on his making Bodoni a Chevalier de la Réunion. This second sum was to be used for the publication of a series of French classics.

Bodoni set out his principles of typography (although stated in vague and general terms) in his *Manuale Tipografico*. This book was completed by his wife who published it in 1818, five years after his death.

The Modern faces of Bodoni and the Didots ousted the old

Bodoni: page from Dante's *La Divina Comedia*, printed in 1796.
(photo: St. Bride Printing Library)

A' STUDIOSI

DEL DIVINO POETA

GIO: JACOPO MARCH. DIONISI

CANONICO DI VERONA.

I

Dalla letterata Firenze, dall'intimo seno
delle sue Biblioteche ho tratta, Signori, con
un po' di destrezza e un po' più di pazienza
nell'anno 1789 la divina Commedia di stra-
niere brutture purgata, e di natíe bellezze
riadorna, la quale or esce felicemente alla
luce. Io la serbava, come cosa cara, per me,
avendo fisso nell'animo di pubblicarla, non
senza le dovute sue illustrazioni, unitamente
alla Vita Nuova, alle Rime, al Convito, e all'

a

style face for most of the nineteenth century. Such types appeared in many poor recuttings and these debased moderns caused a deterioration in the standard of book design. The subsequent revival of interest in earlier faces was a response to this.

Bodoni's faces appear today in two main recuttings: AMERICAN TYPEFOUNDERS' and BAUER. The ATF version was cut by M.F.Benton and copied with minor variations by The MONOTYPE Corporation, HAAS, LINOTYPE, Intertype, and Ludlow, while the more delicate Bauer version is used by Bauer alone. Today, both versions are available in PostScript format.

SR

Chris BRAND   b.1921   B

Albertina (1965) **47**

Chris Brand was born in Utrecht, Belgium, and after studying calligraphy he worked in Brussels from 1948 to 1953. He has taught design and typography in various academies and designed several typefaces of which the best known is Albertina. This was first used for a catalogue of the work of Stanley Morison, which was exhibited at the Albertina Library in Brussels in 1966.

He has also designed a Hebrew font, many book covers, and a title line for a national newspaper.

RCE

Colin BRIGNALL   b.1942   GB

Aachen (1969) **204**
Lightline (1969)
Premier Lightline (1969)
Revue (1969) **612**
Octopuss (1970) **622**
Premier Shaded (1970) **658**
Harlow (1977)
Italia (1977)
Superstar (1977) **509**
Romic (1979) **240**
Corinthian (1981)
Edwardian (1983)

Colin Brignall is Type Director for Esselte LETRASET, an appointment which he has held since 1980. Although primarily a type designer he has also been responsible for many pieces of lettering and logotype design for which he has won various awards.

Born in Warwickshire, he began his career in press photography in London's Fleet Street and eventually went on to spend time in both fashion and commercial photography. In 1964 his experience in commercial photography led him to join Letraset as a photographic technician in their type design studio and it was in this environment that he began to take an interest in letter forms and where he began to experiment with his own ideas in type design.

Among his early works for the Letraset dry transfer range are display styles such as Aachen, Harlow, Premier Shaded, and Superstar. In addition he has designed typefaces suitable for both text and display, including Italia, and Romic, the one-sided serifs of which allowed for the very light letterspacing which was in vogue at the time.

RCE

Neville BRODY   b.1957   GB

Arena/Stadia (1989)
Avanti/Campanile (1989)
Industria (1989)
State (1991)
Typeface Six (1991)
Typeface Seven (1991)

Neville Brody is the best known graphic designer of his generation and his work for *The Face* between 1980 and 1986 revolutionised magazine design worldwide. He grew up in North London, and studied at the London College of Printing. He started his career working on record sleeve designs for a number of companies, and was eventually appointed Art Director of Fetish Records.

Shortly after *The Face* magazine was launched in 1980 he became its Art Director and rapidly turned his attention from image creation to experimentation with type. 'Traditions in typography', he says, 'are not fun—communication should be entertaining!'

His work is characterised by the use of bold typography and many of the logos and much of the display type features hand-drawn letters. The geometric alphabets Typefaces Six and Seven date from this period, and were drawn to replace Futura which had previously been used as the magazine's display type. They have recently been revised and released in

PostScript format.

In 1988 the Victoria & Albert Museum in London hosted an exhibition of his work and the accompanying book *The graphic language of Neville Brody,* was one of the best-selling art books of that year. He is now Art Director of Arena and works for corporate, fashion, music and publishing companies.

RCE

William BULMER   1757–1830   GB
& William MARTIN   GB

Bulmer (1928) **58**

William Martin was the brother of Robert Martin, John BASKERVILLE's foreman. William also trained under Baskerville, whose types clearly influenced his own. Until 1803 they were cut for the exclusive use of William Bulmer's Shakespeare Press in London.

William Bulmer began his career as a printer's apprentice in Newcastle-on-Tyne alongside the engravers Robert Pollard and Thomas Bewick, before going to London where he worked briefly for John BELL. He was set up in business as the Shakespeare Printing Office in 1790 by John Boydell, publisher of engravings, and George Nichol, Bookseller to George III, who both wanted to publish a fine illustrated folio edition of Shakespeare. Meanwhile, in 1786, William Martin came to London and became punch-cutter to George Nicol: Martin's foundry became in effect the private foundry of the Shakespeare Press.

The edition of Shakespeare—known as *The Boydell Shakespeare* appeared in nine volumes between 1792 and 1802 and established the reputation of both Bulmer and Martin.

Martin's types can be described as the last of the transitional faces, and although modelled on Baskerville's, they are taller, narrower and are more sharply cut. D.B.Updike has referred to them as: 'both delicate and spirited, thoroughly English'.

The press also produced a number of other illustrated editions which used Martin's types, the most important being the three-volume *Folio Milton* (1794-07). Two books containing work by his former colleagues in Newcastle were *Poems by Goldsmith and Parnell* (1795), with engravings by Thomas Bewick, and Robert Pollard's *Peerage of Great Britain and Ireland* (1793).

William Bulmer retired in 1821, after taking George

Nichol's son William into the company, and died in 1820. William Martin's types were not used by another printer until McCreery used them for his poem *The Press*, in 1803. If he produced a specimen sheet none has survived, but his types appear on the 1807 specimen of another printer, G.F.Harris.

The current versions of Bulmer are all based on Martin's earlier work, c.1790.

SR

Jackson BURKE   1908-75   USA

Trade Gothic (1948-60) **289**
Majestic (1953-6)
Aurora (1960) **118**

As Director of Typographic Development at Mergenthaler LINOTYPE from 1949 to 1963, Jackson Burke oversaw the production of the typefaces in which the vast majority of American newspapers were set for nearly half a century.

Born in San Francisco, he became an orphan and was brought up by a strict elder sister who ran a boarding school. He was educated in Oregon and the University of California in Berkeley. During World War II he served in the US Navy but was invalided-out before the end while stationed in Hawaii.

After a short period as a private printer at Palo Alto in the Bay area of San Francisco, he joined Mergenthaler Linotype as successor to C.H.GRIFFITH who had been there since 1906, (though not always as Director of Typographic Development). During his time with the company Jackson Burke designed or commissioned a number of new types, including Trade Gothic and the newsprint faces Majestic and Aurora. One of his last responsibilities with the company was the cutting of the Helvetica series.

Apart from typeface development his other achievements at Mergenthaler were threefold. Firstly, he was responsible for the complete development of the newspaper tele-typesetting system (TTS) about which he had reservations, although he saw that it was an economic necessity. Secondly, when photocomposition was developed in the 1950s he insisted on editing or redesigning all the company's newsprint typefaces rather than allow them to be committed to photocomposition without appropriate modification. Thirdly, he extensively developed faces for Indian scripts including various forms of Devanagari, Gujarati and Sinhalese.

He was succeeded at Mergenthaler by Mike PARKER.

RCE

Allesandro BUTTI 1893-1959 I

Paganini (1928) **181**
Landi Echo (1939-43)
Quirinius (1939)
Athenaeum (1945, with Aldo NOVARASE) **134**
Normandia (1946-9, with Aldo Novarase)
Rondine (1948, with Raffaello BERTIERI)
Augustea (1951, with Aldo Novarase) **416, 409**
Fluidum (1951)
Microgramma (1952, with Aldo Novarase)
Cigogna (with Aldo Novarase)

The designer of a diverse range of typefaces many of which have enjoyed wide popular appeal, such as Microgramma and Augustea, both designed with Aldo Novarese for the Italian foundry Nebiolo, (now no longer operating). Rondine and Paganini were designed in conjunction with Raffaello Bertieri.

RCE

Max CAFLISCH b.1916 CH

Columna (1955) **410**

Max Caflisch has been responsible for producing some of the finest book designs of the post-war era and has received International recognition for his work. As a teacher and typographic advisor he is one of the most influential figures of his generation.

He was born at Winterthur in Switzerland and at the age of twelve he visited a printing works and developed a keen interest in what he saw there. Later, from 1932 to 1936, he was apprenticed as a compositor in the printing works of Studer-Schläpfer in Horgen, near Zürich. During this period he attended classes at the famous School of Arts & Crafts in Zürich, where he was noted as an outstanding pupil. Meanwhile, he continued to enrich his knowledge by studying the work of great typographers, particulary the new typography of Jan TSCHICHOLD.

In 1938 he moved to Basel to work as a senior compositor at Benno Schwabe and later Birkhäuser, where Jan Tschichold and Imre REINER were at that time also employed, and remained there until 1941. After a spell of teaching in 1942 at Allgemeiner Gewerbeschule Basel, his most important opportunity came with the printer and publisher Benteli AG in

Bern-Bumpliz where, from 1943 to 1962, he was art director with overall responsibility for all production. At the same time he was busy advising other companies such as Holbein Verlag, Artemis, Francke and Herbert Lang and Staatlicher Lehrmittelverlag Bern.

His work in the field of education began during World War II with the Gewerbeschule (Trade School) in Basel from 1941-1942. Later, in 1962, he was appointed to direct the graphics trade apprenticeship classes at the School of Arts & Crafts in Zürich. During his time there a complete replanning of the graphic department was carried out under his direction. He continued to lecture at the school until 1981 but he also started a further class at the neighbouring Technical School of Graphics Industries, in Zürich, which continued from 1973 to 1978.

In 1955 he created the typeface Columna for the BAUER foundry and later, because of his outstanding knowledge of the technical aspects of typography, he was appointed to advise IBM and the Bauer foundry in Frankfurt on the many aspects of type design associated with computer technology.

Max Caflisch was one of the first to appreciate the need for original alphabets for use with the new digital typesetting technology, and since 1972 he has been responsible for the type design programme at the firm of Rudolf Hell at Kiel, and since 1990 a member of the type advisory board of ADOBE Systems Inc. Despite the fact that a great deal of his present activities are involved with these developments he is still essentially a book designer, a typographer in the truest sense of the word.

RCE

Margaret CALVERT, see KINNEIR

Ron CARPENTER   b.1950   GB

Cantoria (1986)
Calisto (1987) **53A**
Amasis (1990)

Ron Carpenter is senior type designer with the Monotype Corporation. He was born near Dorking, Surrey, and joined Monotype in 1968 where he trained as a typeface draughtsman. In 1975 he became responsible for quality control as a technical checker. His first experience of typeface design came when he assisted Robin NICHOLAS with the italic for his Nimrod. Since assuming his present position in 1984 Ron Carpenter has been responsible for, amongst other typefaces, Cantoria, Calisto and new weights of Times New Roman.

SR

Matthew CARTER   b.1937   GB
& Bitstream Inc.

Snell Roundhand (1966)
Cascade Script (1966)
Gando Ronde (with Hans Jorg Hunziker, 1970)
Olympian (1970) **71**
Auriga (1970) **151**
CRT Gothic (1974)
Video (1977) **283**
Bell Centennial (1978) **284**
Galliard (1978) **74**
V&A Titling (1981)
Bitstream Charter (1987)

Matthew Carter is the son of the printing historian Harry Carter who was archivist to the Oxford University Press and his career has been closely allied to the changes in typesetting and design technology which have taken place over the past thirty years. In 1981 he was elected a Royal Designer for Industry by the Royal Society of Arts.

At nineteen, after leaving school, Matthew Carter spent a year in Holland where he was taught by Jan VAN KRIMPEN's assistant, the punch-cutter P.H.Raedisch. In 1961 he used the skills that he'd acquired to cut a semi-bold for Dante under the direction of John Dreyfus of Monotype and Dante's designer Giovanni MARDERSTEIG. Dante was originally cut by Charles MALIN, who had died in 1955.

Back in London, Carter freelanced for a while before becoming a typographical advisor to Crosfield Electronics, British distributors for the Photon/Lumitype phototypesetting machine. In 1965 he left Crosfield for Mergenthaler LINOTYPE in New York.

Carter stayed with Linotype for six years and even after returning to London he maintained his connection with the company. His Bell Centennial was designed for Linotype, who had been approached for an updated version of Bell Gothic which would be suitable for new technology. (C.H.Griffith of

Linotype had designed the original face for setting American telephone directories but after a switch to CRT systems Bell Gothic reproduced badly.) Carter's replacement typeface was finished in 1978, 100 years after the Bell telephone company produced its first directories, hence its name. Carter's Video and his Olympian family of newspaper types (created for newspapers but revised for more general use in 1981) were both designed to meet the requirements of CRT systems.

Galliard, which Carter designed with Mike PARKER, is based on the types of the seventeenth century punch-cutter Robert GRANJON. It is not a revival in the usual sense of the word, but rather an interpretation of the spirit of Granjon's types, and with its solid weight it has a strength when printed by offset-litho that many old face types lack.

With Parker he set up Bitstream in 1981 to develop and supply digital outline masters for desktop publishing and image setting. It is now one of the largest suppliers of type faces in PostScript format and is also committed to supporting Apple's new TrueType formats. Carter's Bitstream Charter, the first new design to be produced by that company, is influenced by traditional roman types and its italic has some Fournier features.

In addition to the types listed above Carter has designed a number of language types: Hangul (Korean), Rachi Hebrew, Devanagari and several Greeks.

SR

Will CARTER   b.1912   GB

Klang (1955) **328**
Dartmouth (1961)
Octavian (1961, with D.Kindersley) **234**

Will Carter has devoted a lifetime to type design and its execution in a wide variety of print, from the humblest ephemera to the most prestigious commissions.

His entry into the world of type and printing began in a classically direct way. At the age of twelve he accompanied his father on a visit to the Clarendon Press and there met John Johnson who, with encouragement and guidance, let him run off his own visiting cards on a small hand-press. The boy was hooked; and later when Johnson sent him a set of Long Primer No.2 from the biblical composing room at Clarendon, to enable him to 'pursue an amusing and useful hobby', Carter designed and constructed his own crude, hand-press.

A major influence on Carter's development was a visit he made to the studio of the late Rudolf KOCH. Koch had died in 1934 and the studio in those pre-war days was run by his son Paul who had worked extensively with his father as a punch-cutter.

Here Carter met many famous artists including Hermann Zapf whose skill he admired and who was to have a lasting influence on his own work.

In 1949 Carter was drawing closer to achieving his ambition. Circumstances where such that he was able to devote himself entirely to his own printing house, the Rampant Lion Press, which was now commercially self-sufficient. His ideals were simple and direct:

> I was convinced that there was a market for fine jobbing printing of the sort that was too small to be tackled by the big printing houses and yet beyond the scope of the small jobbing firm.

At about this time he designed Klang which was first cut by Monotype in 1955 and which displays the influence of his pre-war calligraphic studies during his visit to the Koch studio. Dartmouth, commissioned by the New England College, was produced in 1961 and Octavian, which he designed with David KINDERSLEY, was produced in 1963.

RCE

The CASLON family   GB
William I   **1692–1766**
William II   **1720–78**
William III   **1754–1833**
William IV   **1780–1869**

Caslon (1725)
the first sans serif (c.1816)

William Caslon I was the first British typefounder of any renown and was responsible for ending the dependence of British printers on imported Dutch types which (with some French types) had dominated the market throughout the seventeenth century.

Born in Worcestershire, William Caslon began his career engraving and chasing gun barrels (occasionally also cutting brass letters for bookbinders) until a printer called William Bowyer, after seeing some of his letters, encouraged him to try punch-cutting. Bowyer was so confident Caslon would succeed he, and two other printers, lent him £500 to start his own foundry whish he opened in Vine Street probably in 1722 or 1723. His first type was possibly a Hebrew, cut for Bowyer around 1722. In the same year he received a commission for a new Arabic fount, from the Society for the Promotion of Christian Knowledge, who wanted to send New Testaments to Palestine and Syria.

His first roman type, the Pica Roman of around 1725 was based closely on a Dutch type owned by the widow of the Amsterdam punch-cutter Dirck Voskens, it was followed two years later by Caslon's English. The foundry moved from Vine Street to Ironmongers' Row in 1727 and during the next two years, three more types appeared: Small Pica No. 1, Long Primer No. 2 and the celebrated Great Primer Roman which was perhaps first used by Sammuel Palmer in Henry Pemberton's *View of Sir Isaac Newton's philosophy* in 1728. An italic for the Great Primer followed in 1730.

In 1734 the foundry moved to Chiswell Street where he published his famous specimen sheet showing almost a full range of the roman types he cut.

Unlike those of the slightly later John Baskerville, Caslon's designs were not innovative—similar types were in use a hundred years earlier—but it was his skills as an engraver that distinguished him and Caslon's, which marks the end of the old face group, became the standard roman for British printers well into the nineteenth century. In 1776 the Oxford University Press felt the need to supplement the celebrated FELL collection of Dutch types with Caslon's roman.

His work found particular favour in America and Caslon type was used by Mary Katherine Goddard of Baltimore for the printing of the Declaration of Independence.

William Caslon I was undoubtedly the most important member of the family and made the greatest contribution to the development of type design; however, the Caslon family continued in the business of typefounding well into the nineteenth century until the death of the last male Caslon in 1873. The foundry continued under their name until 1937.

William Caslon II worked with his father at the Chiswell Street Foundry and took over the business on his father's death in 1766. He continued to manage the business until 1792. His son, William Caslon III, sold his share in the foundry to his mother and sister-in-law in 1792 and with the proceeds purchased Joseph JACKSON's foundry in Salisbury Square (Jackson had died in 1791). In turn he was suceeded by his son William IV, who managed the business from 1807 until 1819 when the foundry was purchased by Blake Garnet & Co. (later to be known as STEPHENSON BLAKE & Co.).

Meanwhile the original Caslon foundry remained in business under Mrs William Caslon II and Mrs Henry Caslon (Henry Caslon had died in 1788) until Henry Caslon II took over in 1809. Under the name of Caslon Son & Livermore, and later H.W.Caslon & Co. Ltd., the foundry remained in existence until 1937 when the matrices and type including the now celebrated Caslon Old Face, were purchased by Stephenson Blake & Co. who thereafter added 'The Caslon Letter Foundry' to their name.

SR/RCE

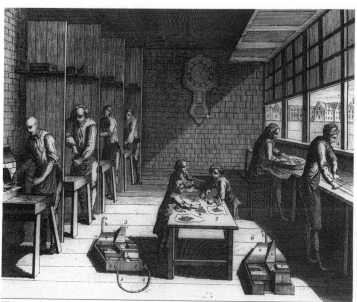

'Engraving of a type foundry presumed to be Caslon's, showing four letter casters at work, four boys breaking off types from surplus metal, a rubber and a dresser. Two halves of enlarged type mould are on the floor'. From *The Universal Magazine*, Vol.vi, 1750.
(photo: St. Bride Printing Library)

A.M.CASSANDRE   1901-68   USSR

Bifur (1929)
Acier Noir (1936)
Peignot (1937)
Touraine (1947, with Charles PEIGNOT)
Cassandre (1968)

A.M.Cassandre was one of the most influential poster artists of the century. Combing his typographic sensitivity with his fine art background, his work is typified by simple, elegant imagery and strong sans serif (capitals-only) lettering. His best examples are considered some of the most enduring examples of the genré.

Born Adolphe Jean-Marie Mouron in Ukraine, his family moved to Paris in 1915 and in 1918 he began to study fine art. To help pay for this he turned to poster design changing his name to avoid any embarrassment. Although now known for his poster work, in the 1940s he was involved in set and costume design for the theatre and, in his later years spent more time oil painting, his first love.

Cassandre's typefaces all reflect his poster work, they were not commissions but personal statements about aspects of typography and communication.

His first typeface Bifur dates from a period when his posters where characterised by the use of capitals-only, sans serif typography. Believing that capitals enhanced the modularity of his work he tried to restore the alphabet to its essential forms. He wrote:

> ...if Bifur looks unfamiliar and strange, it is not because I have dressed it up eccentrically but because, in the midst of a fully clothed crowd it is naked.

Peignot, named after Charles PEIGNOT who commissioned it, is his most famous typeface, and was a reaction to what he saw as the deformation of the lower case alphabet. Peignots' 'lower case' letters are based on capitals with the addition of ascenders as a concession to convention. Despite his reasoning, the lower case was never accepted and later, a revision of the face named Touraine appeared, which had conventional lower-case characters.

After the end of the Second World War his graphic work became more fluid as typified by the Yves Saint Laurent logo drawn in 1963 and still used today. His last typeface design reflects this fluidity, being based on the current architectural forms of the elipse and the trapezoid. It was proposed for the signing for Charles de Gaulle airport in Paris; despite feeling very 'French' it was perhaps too reminiscent of art nouveau and not used. Still unreleased, it was named Cassandre after he took his life in 1968.

PB

William Caxton　1421-91　GB
and the early English printers

William Caxton introduced the art of printing with moveable type to England, where progress in this art had made a relatively slow start. His first types were certainly imported and the standard of his printing was not as good as that of his contemporaries on the continent. In contrast to the lighter roman types of SCHWEYNHEIM & PANNARTZ and JENSON in Italy, Caxton's types were based on the north European blackletter. Caxton was a businessman who became involved in printing when he retired from commerce and engaged himself in translating and publishing.

As a businessman he occupied the important post of Governor of the House of English Merchants at Bruges, then the seat of the Burgundian Court. It was an activity which was to keep him abroad for over 30 years from 1441 and it was during this time that he acquired a knowledge of printing.

He first started printing in 1475 at Bruges, working in partnership with Colard Mansion, a native of Bruges who worked as a calligrapher and translator, and who owned a press. Although most of Colard's books were in French, two were printed for Caxton in English: *Recuyell of the histroryes of Troie* and *The game and the playe of the chesse.* These are the first printed books in the English language.

A year later Caxton returned to England determined to make a success of printing, although he was aware of the financial risks. It is probable that his business activities in Bruges had been less profitable than they might have been because during the whole of his absence abroad, England had been engaged in civil war, a circumstance unlikely to promote trade with other countries. Whatever the reason, he set up a press in London, in Abbey Precinct, Westminster, by the sign of the Red Pale (a sign often adopted by printers in the Netherlands), where in 1477 he produced *The Dictes or Sayengis of the Philosophres,* the first book to be printed in England with a date and place of printing. Although all his early types had been brought from the continent they soon became worn and there is evidence that by 1480 he was using fresh type which had been cut in England; this was in fact his fourth type.

Caxton also printed what is probably the first advertisement printed in England. It consisted of a collection of rules showing how to deal with the concurrence of religious festivals and may well have been displayed publicly in churches throughout England.

When Caxton died in 1491 his types were passed to his foreman, Wynkyn de Worde, who had originally come from Wörth in Alsace and who continued to use them until about 1493, when he developed a type of his own which was probably formed on a French model. He was also the first English printer to print on English-made paper, and until his death in 1535 he concentrated on producing cheaper books in a smaller format.

At about the same time the Oxford Press began with types imported from abroad but later used types resembling Caxton's and thought to be produced by English craftsmen.

Other printers in England at the time included Richard Pynson, a Norman by birth, Julian Notary, who produced several books for Wynkyn de Worde, and the St Albans printer, Lethan & Machlin, about whom little is known. However, their types were crude by comparison with continental types of the period and were a far cry from the high standard of punch-cutting which was to become a feature of English and Scottish typefounding in later centuries.

¶ Here begynneth a lytyll treatyse schortely compyled and called ars moriendi/that is to saye the craft for to deye for the helthe of mannes sowle,

Whan ony of lykylyhode shal deye/thenne is moste necessarye to haue a specyall frende/the whiche wyll hertly helpe and praye for hym & therwyth counseyll the syke for the wele of his sowle/& more ouer to see that alle other so do aboute hym/or ellys quyckly for to make hem departe.¶ Thenne is to be remem

William Caxton, Typeface No.6 for text and Typeface No.8 for heading, from *Ars moriendi*.   (Photo: St. Bride Printing Library)

Warren CHAPPELL   b.1904   USA

Lydian (1938-46) **335**
Trajanus (1940) **10**

Warren Chappell is one of America's most outstanding and versatile figures in the field of type design, graphic art and book illustration, and is also a distinguished writer and editor on the subject of the printed word.

He graduated from the University of Richmond, Virginia, in 1926 and studied under Allen Lewis and George Bridgeman before taking a post in a New York printing office. But his most import training at this time was at Offenbach in Germany where he studied punch-cutting under Rudolf KOCH, who had a powerful influence on many who were to become leading figures in type design in the post-war years. Another important influence was Boardman Robinson with whom Warren Chappell studied illustration at Colorado Springs fine Arts Centre in 1935.

In 1938 he rapidly took the centre stage in America with the design of Lydian, a sans serif face inspired by calligraphic letter forms. Cut for AMERICAN TYPEFOUNDERS', it became one of the most popular typefaces of the period and is still widely used today. His next contribution was Trajanus, a roman letter in the Italian Renaissance style which became available on LINOTYPE. A third type was designed for the Klingspor foundry in 1950 but remained uncut when the foundry merged with the STEMPEL organisation.

Throughout his career Warren Chappell has received wide acclaim as a book designer, and although he has worked for many producers of limited editions, encompassing several hundred titles, the publisher with whom he is most closely associated is Alfred A. Knopf.

RCE

Thomas Maitland CLELAND   1880-1964   USA

Della Robbia/Westminster Old Style (1902) **13**
Garamond (1917 with M.F.Benton)

Thomas Maitland Cleland was a painter, scenic designer, book designer, illustrator and master designer of period typography, who was inspired by the work of William Morris and Will Bradley at the Wayside Press.

Born in Brooklyn, New York, he attended the Artist Artisan

Institute in Chelsea, New York City, before working as a designer at the Caslon Press. He later started his own Cornhill Press in Boston where he met D.B.Updike for whom he undertook design work for the Merrymount Press.

The stone-cut letters of the fifteenth-century Italian sculptor Lucca Della Robbia were the inspiration for the typeface Della Robbia. It was designed for the Bruce Type Company, which in 1902 became part of AMERICAN TYPEFOUNDERS', the organisation for which he worked with M.F.BENTON on the revival, Garamond.

From 1907 to 1908 he was art editor for *McClure's Magazine* and in 1925 worked on the publication *Westvaco Inspirations,* the house journal of the international paper manufacturer, Westvaco Corporation, a post later to be held by Bradbury THOMPSON.

RCE

Thomas J.COBDEN-SANDERSON, see WALKER

Charles Nicolas COCHIN 1715-90 F

Cochin/Moreau-le-jeune/Gravure (1912) **147**

During a life which spanned both the death of Louis XIV and the storming of the Bastille, Charles Nicolas Cochin was in his time one of the greatest influences on the illustrative arts in France and beyond.

He was born into a family of artists in Paris and both his parents were successful engravers, and by the age of 22 Cochin himself was an accomplished artist and engraver.

It was an age of unashamed elegance, of wit rather than wisdom, in which the lesser arts reached new and previously unscaled heights of excellence and one of their most assiduous patrons was Mme de Pompadour, the mistress and friend of the Louis XV. Cochin's talent was soon recognised at court and in 1739, at the age of 24, he was given an important artistic position there. He was also artistic instructor to Mme de Pompadour's younger brother, the Marquis de Marigny, whom he accompanied on the grand tour of Italy between 1749 and 1751.

Like all engravers of his time, Cochin took a special interest in the letter forms used for the text which invariably accompanied an engraving, as the style and execution of these texts was regarded as an important part of the artistic whole. To this end he created a series of graceful alphabets, beautifully in keeping with his style, which for sharpness and elegance were far beyond the realms of anything which could be attempted by typefounders of the day.

Although these alphabets were not bookfaces in the conventional sense they were an important source of inspiration to Baskerville, and later, Didot and Bodoni. The typeface Cochin is a revival issued by Deberny & Peignot.

RCE

COMPUGRAPHIC Corporation USA

Founded in 1960, this American company was acquired by Agfa-Gevaert in 1988 and is now called Agfa Compugraphic. It is the world's largest manufacturer of typesetting equipment and from its offices in Wilmington, Mass, the company also maintains a library of over 1,700 typefaces which includes the entire collection of ITC, as well as many original and redrawn designs commissioned by the company. Compugraphic Lasertype was introduced in 1985 for high quality output on lasersetters, and their library of typefaces is now available in PostScript format.

RCE

Oswald Bruce COOPER 1879-1940 USA

Cooper Old Style (1919-24)
Cooper Black & variants: ~Outline, ~Condensed,
& ~HiLite (1921-26) **467,470**
Cooper Fullface
Cooper Initials
Pompeian Cursive

Oswald Bruce Cooper was a friend of Frederic GOUDY and was part of the circle of artists and designers which met at the Village Press, the private press that Goudy and his wife Bertha ran in Chicago from 1904. Also in the circle were Will Ransom and W.A.DWIGGINS.

In the same year, 'Oz' Cooper formed a partnership with Fred Bertsch called Bertsch & Cooper. The company carried out general typography, newspaper advertisements and book and magazine layouts, with Cooper specializing as a hand lettering artist. In 1913 Cooper had his first notable success when he designed lettering for the Packard Motor Company. The design was considered very original and was granted a design patent and was eventually cut by ATF..

To supplement their lettering and layout services the company added typesetting in 1914 and a year later Cooper designed Cooper Old Style, probably the first type with a rounded serif and the model for many heavy, round-serif types to follow. A companion italic was created in 1924.

Cooper Black was designed in 1925 ('for far-sighted printers with near-sighted customers'), followed by HiLite, a variation with simulated highlights in white. The family was further extended with Cooper Black Condensed and Cooper Black Italic in 1925 and 1926.

RCE

Freeman CRAW   b.1917   USA

Craw Clarendon (1955-60)
Craw Modern (1958-64) **164**
Ad Lib (1961)
Canterbury
Chaucery
Classic
Cursive
GBS Sans

As well as being an important contributor to typeface design Freeman Craw has also been a major figure in the creation of complete visual identity programmes for some of the world's leading companies. For more than ten years he has been Vice-President and art director of Tri-Arts Press during which he has been responsible for the complete graphic control of some of the most impressive printed material in America.

His early typefaces were designed for AMERICAN TYPE-FOUNDERS', but in the past 20 years his designs have been primarily associated with photocomposition.

RCE

Wim CROUWEL   b.1928   NL

New Alphabet (1967)
Fodor Alphabet (1969)

Wim Crouwel was born in Groningen where he studied at the local Academy of Arts & Crafts and later at the Institute of Arts & Crafts in Amsterdam. In 1952 he started his own design studio and in 1963, with Frisco Kramer, Paul Schwartz and Benno Wissing, founded Total Design—the first group of its kind in the Netherlands—a group which undertook major projects for the Amsterdam Airport Authority and the Dutch postal and telecommunications services.

An ardent supporter of lower-case typography he proposed a single-alphabet typeface following the introduction of electronic typesetting devices. Some of the characters bore no resemblance to existing ones and although it was the subject of much attention it was not taken up with any seriousness. Two years later, in 1969, he created Fodor Alphabet, a typeface designed for use in the posters and catalogues of Amsterdam's Fodor Museum.

From 1965 to 1978 he taught at Delft University and was professor there from 1972 to 1978. For a time he was design consultant to the Stedelijk Museum in Amsterdam and is currently Director of Museum Boymans-van Beningen in Rotterdam.

RCE

DEBERNY & PEIGNOT FOUNDRY, see PEIGNOT family

Ernst F.DETTERER, see MIDDLETON

Sjoerd Hendrik DE ROOS   1877-1962   NL

A Javanese Type (1909)
Mediæval/Hollandse Mediæval (1912) **3**
Ella Cursive (1915)
Zilver Type (1915)
Erasmus Mediæval (1923) **2**
Meidoorn Roman (1927)
Grotius (1925)
Egmont (1933) **157**
Nobel (1935)
Libra (1938) **378**
Simplex (1939)
De Roos (1947) **108**

In the sixteenth century Holland was the world centre of type founding but when Sjoerd Hendrik de Roos was engaged by the Amsterdam Letter Foundry in 1907 it had been many years since that country had originated any new type designs.

De Roos was born in Drachten, in the province of Friesland. He tried his hand at many areas of design before settling on type. He trained as a decorative artist and was, variously, a lithographer, portrait painter, landscape artist and designer of furniture. He joined the Amsterdam Letter Foundry (Lettergieteij Amsterdam) as a designer and was later made its artistic head, a position he held for thirty five years.

De Roos became part of the revival of interest in typography then taking place in Britain and the United States and the export of his types raised the profile of Dutch printing. He admired the work of Bruce Rogers and D.B.Updike, while maintaining his own individual style. He specialised in free adaptations of historic faces rather than pure revivals.

His most popular type was the Egmont family, a light-faced roman with strikingly short descenders. Both Simplex and Libra are attempts at single-alphabet types but, as uncials, they have nothing in common with the modernist proposals of either BAYER or SCHWITTERS. His last type, De Roos Roman, was designed during the war and cut on his retirement. It was much used by printers of Dutch fine editions.

SR

abcd

efghijkl

S.H.De Roos, Erasmus Mediæval, 1923.
(Photo: St. Bride Printing Library)

Theodore Low DE VINNE 1828-1914 USA

Century (1894, with Linn Boyd Benton) **62**

Theodore Low De Vinne was America's greatest scholar-print-
er. He was the son of a Londonderry Irish immigrant who
became a Methodist minister, and who was educated enough
to teach his son Greek and Latin. Starting as a compositor De
Vinne rose to the highest levels of his profession, and in the
process his career spanned every advance in printing from
the hand-press to the cylinder press, and from hand-composi-
tion to machine composition.

After serving his apprenticeship he worked as a compositor for Henry Hart of Francis Hart & Co and later became a
junior partner in the firm. When Henry Hart died De Vinne
purchased the whole of the company and changed the name
to Theodore L.De Vinne & Co. De Vinne was responsible for
the production of the *Century* Magazine and collaborated in
the production of Century, the typeface which was specially
cut for it by Linn Boyd BENTON. The typeface was later revised
by Linn Boyd Benton's son, Morris Fuller Benton, who produced some eighteen variations on it, of which Century
Schoolbook is one.

As well as being a practical printer he was also a distinguished writer and from the age of about 28 he began to write
about the historical and practical aspects of print. One of his
most important books is *The Invention of Printing,* in which he
set out to show that the invention of moveable type was the
work of Johann GUTENBERG. Another work, *Plain Printing Types,*
is the fruit of his long study of typefounders' specimen books.

RCE

The DIDOT family   F
François   1689-1757
François-Ambroise   1730-1804
Pierre-François   1732-93
Pierre   1761-1853
Firmin   1764-1836

Didot Floriated Capitals (c.1820)
Neo-Didot (1904) **180**
Didot (1908) **156**

The Didot family of Paris dominated the French book world in
the late eighteenth and early nineteenth centuries. Its mem-

bers were involved in printing, publishing, type founding, punch-cutting and paper manufacture. However the most important member of the family as far as type design is concerned was Firmin Didot, the grandson of the founder, who is generally agreed to have produced the first modern face in 1784 and as a result Didot roman types became standard book types used in France during the nineteenth century and are still in general use today.

The printing dynasty began with François Didot who was a bookseller before he started his own printing works. His son François-Ambroise took over the original business and worked there with his brother Pierre-Françoise until 1789 when Pierre-François left to set up a printing office of his own, and later a paper mill. Inspired by Baskerville in England Pierre-François was to use this mill to produce the first French wove paper.

Both men enjoyed royal patronage: François-Ambroise Didot was printer to the Compte d'Artois who was later to become Charles IX while his brother Pierre was printer to the Compte de Provence, later to become Louis XVIII. As a result of François-Ambroise Didot's reputation, Benjamin Franklin sent his grandson to him to learn punch-cutting. François-Ambroise was also the Director of the Imprimerie National and in this capacity he revised FOURNIER's point system. His name survives in the continental Didot Point.

François-Ambroise Didot initially printed with Garamond types but later began to produce his own. The exact date for this change is uncertain but 1775 has been put forward by D.B.Updike among others. Certainly a new Didot type, a light transitional roman, was in use in 1782 and was used the following year in three quarto editions of French classics.

In 1783 François-Ambroise' son Firmin, then nineteen, took over from his father's previous punch-cutter Pierre Louis Wafflard. In the following year he produced the first modern face which appeared in an edition of Tasso's *Gerusalemme Liberata*. It is characterised by thin serifs, a marked vertical stress and abrupt shading from thick strokes to thin. By this time the Didots were using wove paper and an improved printing press which allowed the fine details of such type to be reproduced.

Firmin took over the foundry when his father retired in 1789, and continued to produce new types. He favoured neo-classical designs with increasingly fine hair serifs. Meanwhile his older brother, Pierre acquired the printing half of the business, but each was to branch out into the other's area so that Firmin also printed and Pierre acquired a foundry in 1809, he later aquired the BASKERVILLE types although he did not use them.

The two brothers also worked together on a series of fine editions illustrated by contemporary artists which they called *Editions du Louvre.* In 1811 Firmin was made Printer to the Institute Francais and Royal Printer in 1814. He retired in 1827 leaving his sons Ambroise-Firmin and Hyacinth to continue the business.

Pierre, the uncle of Firmin, was succeeded by his own sons Henri Didot (typefounder and punch-cutter), Didot St-Legér (who took over the mill) and 'Didot jeune' (a typefounder). Didot St-Legér was responsible for introducing the paper making machine to France. Henri is notable for cutting a miniature type, $2^1/_2$ pt, when he was 66.

Two Monotype revivals of Didot's 1784 type exist, Didot and Neo Didot. Another Didot based type is WALBAUM. This was cut in the early nineteenth century and revived by Oliver Simon for the Curwen Press in 1925.

SR

Walter J.DIETHELM   b.1913   CH

Diethelm Roman (1948-50)
Sculptura (1957)

Walter Diethelm was Art Director for the Swiss typefoundry, HAAS. He trained at the School of Arts & Crafts, Zürich, at the Académie Rauson and, with Ferdinand Léger, at the Grande Chaumière in Paris. For ten years he was art director for a major printing company in Zürich. He now runs his own design studio which he started in 1954. His book *Signet Signal Symbol* has won wide acclaim in the advertising world.

RCE

Dick DOOIJES   b.1909   NL

Rondo (1948, with Stephan Schlesinger)
Mercator (1957-61) **280**
Contura (1966) **418**
Lectura (1966) **83**
Bronletter

A critic and typographer as well as a type designer, Dick Dooijes won the City of Amsterdam's prize for typography for his work on the book *De Letter als Kuntswerk (The Letter as a Work of Art)*.

Dick Dooijes learnt type designing at the Amsterdam Letter Foundry from S.H.DE ROOS. Dooijes was de Roos's assistant for a time and worked with him on the designs for Egmont and De Roos Roman. Dooijes Lectura is a loose adaptation of the sixteenth-century Dutch faces which William CASLON had used as the models for his own types. Mercator is based on the nineteenth-century grotesks. Dooijes added to Rondo, a face principally designed by Stephan Schlesinger. His Bronletter is a private design commissioned for the printers Gooi & Stickl.

An essay he wrote on de Roos accompanied the 1976 exhibition *Three Times De Roos* in The Hague.

SR

William Addison DWIGGINS   1880-1956   USA

Metro (1929-30) **263**
Electra (1935-49) **148**
Caledonia/Cordelia (1938) **174**
Eldorado (1951)

W.A.Dwiggins was a graphic artist who began designing types when he was 44 at the invitation of Mergenthaler LINOTYPE. His first type was a san serif, Metro. His best known face is Caledonia which fuses aspects of the Scotch Romans and the types cut for Bulmer by William Martin.

Dwiggins had a varied career that took in illustration, printing, advertising and book design. After working as a freelance designer he was made Acting Director of the Harvard University Press, 1917-18. He was a skilled calligrapher; in 1919 while living in Boston, Mass, he founded the Society of Calligraphers, Boston, and he used his own calligraphic lettering for the jackets of books he designed. He wrote widely on design matters; Mergenthaler Linotype's idea for a Dwiggins sans serif came from reading him on sans serif faces in one of his books *Layout in Advertising*.

Dwiggins was a friend of another late entrant to type design, Frederic GOUDY. Dwiggins studied lettering under Goudy in Chicago while a student at Frank Holme's School of Illustration. When Goudy moved to Hingham, Mass., Dwiggins followed and was to work there for the rest of his life. He built a puppet theatre at his home for which he wrote plays, made puppets and sets and gave shows under the name of Dr Hermann Puterschein.

In 1929 he was awarded the American Institute of Graphic Arts Gold Medal.

SR

The ELZEVIR family   NL
Louis I   1540-1617
Bonaventura   1583-1652
Abraham I   1592-1652
Isaac   1596-1651

The first Elzevir printing press was set up at Leyden in 1618 by Isaac Elzevir. Until that time, although the family had established a very successful publishing business, all their printing had been done by others. Louis Elzevir, Isaac's grandfather, had fled to Leyden from Antwerp in 1580 to escape the religious disturbances in the Low Countries and after working for the printer Christopher PLANTIN for a short period, had conceived a plan to set up bookshops in every centre of learning in Europe.

Isaac, the first master printer in the family, became printer to the University of Leyden in 1620 and was responsible for introducing the small format books for which the family were to become famous throughout Europe. When Isaac retired in 1625 the business continued under Bonaventura and his nephew Abraham and in the next 25 years the small format editions, known as 'Elzevirs', were pre-eminent in Europe with the new class of readers that had sprung up as a result of the religious disputations of the time.

Although not considered to be the greatest examples of book production, 'Elzivirs' undoubtedly met a growing need for low-priced books at a time when books generally were beyond the pocket of most students and scholars. They were intended for book-readers rather than book-lovers, and the far-sightedness of the founder, Louis Elzevir, was rewarded long after his death when the Elzevir family business enjoyed a dominant position in the book trade of Europe for almost a century.

During the nineteenth century the name Elzevir was perpetuated on the continent as a type description meaning any roman letter not of the Didot kind. In 1852, for example, shortly after the revival of Caslon in the UK, Alexandre de Berny, one of the original founders of the company which would later be known as Deberny & Peignot, introduced a roman showing many of the modifications associated with

he term old style. Similar types offering relief from the Didot
nodels were designed by the Lyons publisher Louis Perrin,
ind the name Elzevir was applied to these types generally
)ecause it evoked the classical period of European printing.

RCE

EMIGRÉ FONTS,
see LICKO

Jakob ERBAR   1878-1935   D

Feder Grotesk (1910)
Erbar **253** & variants:
Lucina, Lumina, Lux & Phosphor (1922-30)
  Koloss (1923) **479**
  Candida (1936) **191**

Jakob Erbar spent most of his life in Cologne working and
teaching at the Kîlner Werkschule. In 1910 he designed his
first type, Feder Grotesk, and went on to create a number of
typefaces for the Frankfurt typefounders Ludwig & Mayer.
The best of known of these is the one which bears his name,
Erbar; one of the first geometric sans serifs it pre-dates both
Paul RENNER's Futura and Rudolf KOCH's Cable.

RCE

SUPER
£25.!?

Jakob Erbar's Phosfor.

ESSELTE LETRASET,
see LETRASET

Roger EXCOFFON 1910–1983 F

Chambord (1937)
Mistral (1953) **322**
Choc (1955)
Diane (1956)
Calypso (1958) **688**
Antique Olive (1962–66) **271**

Born in Marseilles, Roger Excoffon is rightly associated with the 'nouvelle vague' and all that was exuberant in post-war French advertising design. Like many creators of type in the twentieth century he approached his subject from the standpoint of graphic design and in doing so achieved a subtle blend of eloquence and economy which perfectly suited the mood of the period.

After university education at Aix-en-Provence where he read law with little enthusiasm, Roger Excoffon went to Paris to study painting, but here his preference turned increasingly towards graphic art and the design of letter forms. In 1947 he formed his own advertising agency in Paris, the highly successful U & O, and at about the same time he became Design Director of a small but ambitious Marseilles type foundry, Fonderie Olive. This was an appointment which was to prove an exceptionally fruitful one both for Roger Excoffon and the foundry's proprietor, Maurice Olive.

As a freelance he had already worked for the Fonderie Olive and had designed Chambord, a typeface modeled on CASSANDRE's Peignot, but in his position as Design Director new typefaces appeared rapidly and to enthusiastic acclaim. In addition, he helped in the design of another type, François GANEAU's Vendôme, which was modelled on seventeenth-century French types.

Between 1962 and 1966 he designed his most successful face, Antique Olive (Antique is French for sans serif). It was a response to the increasing demand for sans serif faces following the sucess of HAAS' Helvetica and DEBERNY & PEIGNOT's Univers which were intended to give the clean contemporary (some would say lifeless) look of the 60s.

These new and exiting faces gave French advertising and graphic design much of the vigour and exuberance for which it was acclaimed at the time. The work for Air France and Bally Shoes are typical of the genre: stylish and modernistic, it became the standard of excellence for the period, and even today its freshness and economy—largely the result of the new typefaces—is still apparent.

RCE

Alfred FAIRBANK 1895-1982 GB

Narrow Bembo Italic (1923)

Undoubtedly the man who did more than any other to revive the use of the italic cursive hand. A brilliant calligrapher himself, he was renowned as a teacher and writer on handwriting and his *Handwriting Manual* is considered to be the definitive work on the subject.

He was also a type designer and his Narrow Bembo Italic has been much admired. Although he would have liked to create more usable types, it was unfortunate that he lived at a period when, in England at least, carvers rather than calligraphers were preferred as type designers.

RCE

Fell types re-cast for H.Hart's *Notes on a century of typography at the University Press, Oxford 1693-1794*, 1900.   (Photo: St. Bride Printing Library)

.... My ſon, be admoniſhed : of making many books

Dr John FELL 1625-86 GB

Fell Types (c.1672)

Dr Fell was a Bishop of Oxford, Dean of Christ Church and Vice-Chancellor of Oxford University. Between 1670 and 1672 he imported types, punches and matrices which were bought in Holland on his behalf by Thomas Marshall. These included some GRANJON types and some supplied by VAN DIJCK. With three others (and for an annual payment of £200) he took over the management of the University Press in 1672. In 1676 he set up a type foundry, attached to the press and employing a Dutch type-cutter Peter Walpergen, a specimen sheet was publishedin 1693.

The types cast from his collection, known as the Fell types, became neglected until their revival by C.H.O.Daniel at his private press from 1877 onwards. In 1915 Francis Meynell persuaded the controller of Oxford University Press to let him have two cases of Fell type with which Meynell and Morison printed two books.

Fell is the subject of the well known epigram by Tom Brown:

> I do not like thee, Dr Fell
> The reason why I cannot tell;
> But this I know, I know full well
> I do not like thee, Dr Fell

SR

Vincent FIGGINS   1766-1844   GB

Gresham (1792, re-issued 1925)
Figgins Shaded (c.1815, re-issued 1937)
Egyptian (1817)

Vincent Figgins was one of the influential early nineteenth-century typefounders working in London and was responsible for the introduction of the first egyptian typeface in 1817.

He started at the age of sixteen as an apprentice in the foundry of Joseph Jackson in London and because of the declining health of his master the management of the foundry fell increasingly on his shoulders. When Joseph Jackson died in 1792, Figgins was well qualified to take over the business but lack of finance made this impossible and the entire foundry was purchased by William Caslon III.

Figgins was determined to succeed on his own and with some help from John Nichols, who had been a friend of Joseph Jackson, he was eventually able to start his own business in Swan Yard, Holborn Bridge, London.

One of his most important commissions was the production of a facsimile type for Macklin's Bible for which Jackson had originally cut the type in 1789. When the printer Bensley had partly completed the work he decided to renew the type and chose not to go to Caslon, who now held the Jackson matrices, but instead asked Figgins to cut a font to correspond with the original. Figgins obliged by cutting a perfect match: a type which was later used for a number of important publications including Thomson's *Seasons* of 1797. The reputation of Figgins was now well established and a succession of

From Figgins' *Specimen of printing types,* 1833.
(Photo: St. Bride Printing Library)

FOUR-LINE EMERALD SANS-SERIF SHADED.

MONMOUTHSHIRE

TWO-LINE LONG PRIMER SHADED, No. 3.

ENTERTAINMENT

roman types followed, for both English and Scottish printers. He was also successful with newspaper types which were also undergoing radical changes with the introduction of the steam press: one of the first was adopted by The Times in 1814.

It is for his work with display types, however, that he is chiefly remembered. His later specimen books showed that he could compete with the new foundries such as STEPHEN-SON BLAKE by producing a range of powerful display types, including the very first egyptians (named after his original typeface), which matched the new mood of the industrial revolution. This first truly original design of advertising type was brought out in 1817; with its heavy, slab serifs and even weight it has been described as a typical expression of the machine age.

RCE

Karl Erik FORSBERG   b.1914   S

Parad (1936)
Lunda (1938)
Berling (1951-58) **45**
Carolus
Ericus

Karl Erik Forsberg (pronounced Forsh'berry), a Swede, trained in typography, calligraphy and as a compositor in Basel, Switzerland, a combination which, not surprisingly led him to design types. He worked for Almquist and Wiksell as head designer before becoming head of another Swedish publishing company P.A.Norsted and Sons, where he succeeded Akke Kumlien.

Berling is his best known typeface. It was called after the

foundry that produced it, Berlingska Stilgjuteriet of Lund. Berling was first used in the *Rembrandt Bible,* so called because it is illustrated with works by Rembrandt. This bible won an award for the most beautiful book of the year on its publication in 1954. Forsberg's Carolus and Ericus are alphabets of capitals, while Lunda was designed for use in advertising.

Forsberg's other work includes covers for books and magazines, also designs for postage stamps. With Akke Kumlien (designer of the typeface of that name) he set up the School for Graphic Design in Stockholm.

SR

Pierre Simon FOURNIER ('le jeune')   1712-68   F

Fournier (1925) **90**
Barbou (1968) **89**

Pierre Simon Fournier, also known as Fournier le jeune, made several important contributions in the field of type design. He set up his own foundry in Paris where he cut and founded all the types himself, pioneered the concept of the type family and is said to have cut 60,000 punches for 147 alphabets of his own design. He created new printers' flowers and ornaments that caught the mood of his age. He broke a monopoly on music printing in France and improved existing methods of printing music. He also invented a point system for standardising music type and published its first version when he was only 25. (The DIDOT system used on the Continent today was developed from Fournier's and retained the name of his unit, 'the point', while fractionally altering its size). Not surprisingly perhaps, Fournier's death at 56 was attributed to overwork.

Pierre Simon Fournier was the youngest son of a printing family. His father Jean Claude Fournier of Auxerre worked for the great founder Guillaume Le Bé and took over management of the foundry for Le Bé's daughters after his death. This foundry, with its extensive collection of historic types, was later bought by the eldest of Jean Claude's sons, Jean Pierre (also known as Fournier l'aîné, or the elder). The middle brother François was a printer.

Pierre Simon studied watercolour painting with the miniaturist J.B.G.Colson but became involved in type design through work which he did for his eldest brother. He started off engraving woodblocks and large capitals, later moving on to fonts of type. In 1736 he began his own foundry, and pub-

Pierre Simon Fournier, frontispiece to *Manuel typographique,* vol i, 1764. (photo: St. Bride Printing Library)

lished the first version of his point system the following year. In 1742 he published a specimen book, printed by Jean Joseph Barbou, part of a long association between the two men.

The two main influences on Fournier's types were the celebrated Romains du Roi cut by GRANDJEAN for the Imprimerie Royale in 1702, and the narrow letters favoured in Holland and Germany. This resultant type had condensed proportions and the capitals were the same height as the ascenders of the lower-case. His sharply-cut types were produced in a number of styles: ordinaire, goût Hollandáis, poétique etc. Such styles were not intended as separate faces but as part of a type family in the same way as a modern founder might offer one face in light, bold, semi-bold, condensed and so on. Fournier's italic is generally agreed to be a more innovative face than his romans. He called attention to its difference from the italics of the past. He had made it more like the hand of the eighteenth-century French engravers, had increased stroke contrast and introduced serifs on some lower-case letters though in this last point he may have been following the lead of Grandjean's successor Louis Luce. (Luce certainly felt another Fournier type style, his condensed 'poetique', owed too much to his own work).

For much of his life Fournier lived in the Place Estrapade in Paris in a house once occupied by Philippe Grandjean.

Fournier took a keen interest in the history and theory of printing and typography and wrote several papers on aspects of these subjects. His most famous work is the two-volume *Manuale Typographique* dated 1764 and 1766 (though the second volume was actually published in 1768).

He is probably best remembered as the designer of one of the early transitional faces. His St Augustin Ordinaire served as the model for the Monotype transitional face Fournier released in 1925. Another version of this face, Barbou, was cut by Monotype at the same time, in 13D/14pt. Although used in *The Fleuron* no.7, in 1930, it was not released to the trade until 1968, the bicentenary of Fournier's death.

SR

Benjamin FOX,
see THORNE & THOROWGOOD

Adrian FRUTIGER b.1928 CH

Phoebus (1953)
Ondine (1954) **336**
President (1954)
Univers (1957) **267/481/498**
Opera (1959-60)
Egyptienne (1960) **210,**
Apollo (1964) **133**
Serifa (1967) **198/518**
OCR-B (1968) **304**
Iridium (1975) **149**
Frutiger (1976) **266/489**
Breughel (1982) **113**
Icone (1982) **223**
Versailles (1982)
Centennial (1986) **187A**

Adrian Frutiger is one of the most important type designers to emerge since World War II. He is the designer of many notable faces—the best known being the sans serifs Univers and Frutiger—and was one of the first designers to create type for film composition.

Frutiger, who now lives just outside Paris, was born in Switzerland in 1928 near Interlaken. He was apprenticed in that town to printers Otto Schaeffli as a compositor, after his father refused his request to be allowed to train as a sculptor. Frutiger has said that his liking for sculpture has persisted throughout his career and finds expression in the types he designs. During his apprenticeship he learnt woodcutting and wrote, illustrated, engraved and produced a small book about local churches. Between 1948 and 1951 Frutiger studied at the School of Fine Arts in Zürich where his subjects included calligraphy. Charles PEIGNOT recruited Frutiger for Deberny & Peignot after seeing a brochure he had produced, *History of Letters,* which used his wood engraving skills.

The founders Deberny & Peignot were connected with the Lumitype/Photon photosetting machine and needed faces adapted to suit it. Charles Peignot wanted Frutiger to adapt Futura and this provided the impetus for Univers. Frutiger found Futura too geometric for his taste, he also wanted to create a large, matched family of faces of different weights. The twenty-one members of the Univers family have five weights and four widths, and were all designed before the first matrix was struck. They were numbered to make selection easy, but other founders who supplied the new type did not adopt his system. Many founders followed Deberny & Peignot and produced large sans serif type families of their own. Haas for instance developed Helvetica.

Although Frutiger has said that all his types have Univers as their skeleton he felt, when he came to design a face for the Charles de Gaulle Airport at Roissy, that Univers seemed dated, with a 1960s feel. His airport face, originally known as Roissy but renamed Frutiger for its issue to the trade by Mergenthaler LINOTYPE in 1976, is a humanistic sans serif that has been compared to GILL and JOHNSTON types.

Frutiger has created a broad range of typefaces including OCR-B a type for optical character recognition. His 1982 Breughel is an original face almost wholly comprised of curves and fitting into no existing type category. He has embraced new technology and used it to advantage in faces such as Centennial, a modern whose fine serifs are made possible by recent improvements in definition. More than ten years earlier his Iridium had demonstrated that the classical modern face was neither outdated nor necessarily caused legibility problems. Frutiger himself is sceptical about theories of legibility. He learnt to read with gothic characters without difficulty and says legibility is solely a matter of habit.

In 1986 Adrian Frutiger received the Gutenberg prize for technical and aesthetic achievement in type.

SR

Joseph FRY   1728-87   GB
& the Fry Foundry

Fry's Baskerville (1768) **54**
Old Face Open (1788, re-issued 1928)

Joseph Fry established the Fry foundry which was later taken over by his two sons. London's Type Street (now Moore Street) was so called because it became home to the Fry Foundry.

Trained for the medical profession, Joseph Fry was inspired to take up typefounding by the example of BASKERVILLE and there are some similarities between the two men. Fry, like Baskerville, was a Birmingham man by birth who came to typefounding relatively late in his career having been successful in other fields. Among his numerous business ventures he started Fry's Chocolates.

In 1764, while living in Bristol, Fry decided to go into partnership with a local printer, William Pine, and set up a foundry attached to Pine's print works. Isaac Moore, previously a whitesmith (that is, a metal finisher), was taken on to cut types for them and later became a partner. Moore cut his types after Baskerville's, though they're not close copies, and the foundry's early types are all of this kind. In 1766 they published their first specimen sheet and two years later the firm moved to London as Isaac Moore and Company, one of many renamings.

In 1770 they published another specimen sheet which shows a much more extensive selection of types sizes than their first and a number of ornaments. In 1776 Moore retired and the foundry produced CASLON style types in preference to Baskerville's. With the advent of the modern face both these styles of type would be melted down and recast.

Fry's two sons Edmund and Henry joined the firm in 1782 and in 1787 Fry retired and died shortly after.

Dr Edmund Fry, the eldest son, had trained as a doctor but was too deaf to practice. He was famous for his scholarship and when he ran the foundry he concentrated on founding and acquiring learned language types. His philological work, *Pantographia,* contained over two hundred alphabets. In 1827 he created a type for the blind (not braille but raised letters, all uppercase). In 1828 Edmund retired and sold his stock to William THOROWGOOD of Fann Street.

SR

Johann FUST, see GUTENBERG

François GANEAU 1912-80 F

Vendôme (1951-54) **31**

François Ganeau was born in Paris and was principally a sculptor and theatre decorator with numerous public commissions to his credit after World War II. He was a friend of Maurice Olive, the proprietor of the Fonderie Olive in Marseille where Roger EXCOFFON was the chief designer. François Ganeau's typeface Vendôme was cut at the Fonderie Olive in 1951-54. It is possible that Roger Excoffon assisted in the design of this face.

RCE

Claude GARAMOND c.1500-61 F

Grecs du Roi (c.1549)
[Garamond/Garamont/Garaldus (1912/1930/1956 see
JANNON/GOUDY/NOVARESE)] **91-96**
[Granjon (1928)] **66**

Claude Garamond's roman letters, designed at his Paris foundry, took the roman of Aldus MANUTIUS as their model and were much copied. By the end of the sixteenth century they had become the standard European type and they were still in use in the eighteenth century.

Little is known of his early life, but he may have worked with several punch-cutters before embarking on a career of his own. In the late 1520s he was approached by the scholar

Claude Garamond. (Photo: St. Bride Printing Library)

and printer Robert Estienne to cut types, and Garamond's first roman appears in the 1530 edition of *Paraphrasis in Elegantiarum Libros Laurentii Vallae* by Erasmus.

The model Garamond used for this type was the 1455 *De Aetna* roman of Aldus Manutius, but Garamond refined the type to suit his own tastes.

Following the success of his roman, the King, François I, commissioned a greek, now known as the Grecs du Roi, for his exclusive use.

In 1545 Garamond began publishing on his own account using types of his own design including a new italic cut in two sizes. His first book was the *Pia et Religiosa Meditatio* of David Chambellan.

After Garamond's death in 1561 his punches and matrices were sold off, a principle buyer was Christopher PLANTIN of Antwerp, but type also found its way to Frankfurt where it appeared in a 1592 specimen of the Egenolff-Bermer foundry.

Garamond's types have been much revived this century and several versions exist under his name, most however are based on the Caractères de l'Université in the Imprimerie Royale (the Royal Printing Office, in Paris). In 1925, Beatrice Warde (under her pseudonym Paul Beaujon) proved these to be the work of the later Jean JANNON.

The most accurate revival of a Garamond-style type is G.W.JONES's Granjon of 1928-31, which was so named to avoid confusion with all the other Garamonds.

SR

Arthur Eric Rowton GILL   1882-1940   GB

Gill Sans (1927-30) **259, 424-8, 476, 527**
Golden Cockerel Press Type (1929)
Perpetua (1929-30) **116, 438**
Solus (1929)
Joanna (1930-31) **111**
Aries (1932)
Floriated Capitals (1932) **538**
Bunyan/Pilgrim (1934) **183**
Cunard/Jubilee (1933/4)

Eric Gill, a leading Catholic, pacifist, socialist and social critic of his time—as well as letter-cutter, sculptor, wood-engraver and type designer—was one of the most prominent and contraversial figures of his day. His writings concerned social reform: the integration of craftsmanship and industry, art and religion and flesh and spirit, but nothing in his own life was straight-forward. His condemnation of industrial manu-facture would be undermined by his work for Monotype, and his religous beliefs by his sexual appetite and adventures. Over fifty years after his death, it is his typefaces for which he is chiefly remembered.

Gill was born in Brighton in 1882, the son of a noncon-formist minister. He studied at Chichester School of Art before being apprenticed to the ecclesiastical architect W.D. Caroe in London. While in London he attended classes taught by the calligrapher Edward JOHNSTON at the Central School of Arts & Crafts where later he reported being 'struck, as by lightening'. The two became firm friends and Gill shared rooms with Johnston for a while in nearby Lincolns Inn. Through Johnston he became involved in the small world of scribes and illuminators and the larger world of the Arts & Crafts movement, it gave him direction, he gave up his job and embarked on a career as a stone-cutter and letterer.

He always regarded himself as a workman and, after his marriage to Ethel Moore in 1904, went to live in a block of workers' flats in Battersea. In 1905 they moved to Hammer-smith, home to William MORRIS in his most revolutionary phase, and a haven of the private press movement. A few doors away, in Emery WALKER's old house, was Edward John-ston, and though both he and Gill were still close, the rela-tionship was changing away from the dependance of pupil on teacher.

Gill's work at this time was varied: inscriptions, tomb-stones, head-peices and initial letters for private presses, including Emery Walker's Doves Press and Harry Kessler's Cranach Press in Weimar. The calligraphic influence of John-ston, while still present in Gill's lettering, was beginning to be secondary to ideas of his own, drawn from the practical nature of his work and the physical restrictions of his tools.

The Gills left Hammersmith in 1907 and set up the first of their three craft-based, self-sufficient religious communities. (The others were at Capel-y-ffin in Wales, 1924-28 and Pigotts in Buckinghamshire, 1928-40.) They were converted to Catholicism in 1913, Ethel changing her name to Mary. Short-ly afterwards he began work on the *Stations of the Cross* in West-minster Cathedral, fourteen low-relief sculptures with lettering combined, perhaps the very best of his sculptures.

Gill designed his first typeface at the invitation of Stanley MORISON of the MONOTYPE Corporation. The drawings for this

Mr Eric Gill painted, and affixed with his own hands, the name-plate of the most renowned train of our day, the "Flying Scotsman".'
From the *Monotype Recorder,* Winter 1933.
(Photo: St. Bride Printing Library)

type, Perpetua, were begun in 1925. Morison had made the request because he felt Gill's background in cutting stone inscriptions would give him an understanding of serifs. Charles MALIN, who had worked for the French foundry DEBERNY & PEIGNOT, cut the type before the work was passed to the Monotype works for production. Perpetua takes its name from the first book in which it was used (in its first size), *The Passion of Perpetua & Felicity,* 1928. The original italic, cut in 1930, was called Felicity, but is not the same as the finally released Perpetua italic.

Gill Sans, designed during the same period, was based on the same sources as Johnston, though Gill distinguished the two faces by saying that his own was designed to be read as a text face whereas Johnston's was intended purely for signs. Gill had used san serif lettering for signs in his at Capel-y-Ffin and for the lettering on a Bristol Bookshop owned by Douglas Cleverdon which Gill painted in 1927. It was this bookshop sign which suggested the idea of a Gill sans serif to Morison.

Joanna, was named after his daughter Joan and designed for Hague & Gill, the printing partnership formed by Gill and Joan's husband René Hague. It was cut by the CASLON foundry and one of its first uses in 1931 was for Gill's own *Essay on typography.* In 1938 J.M.Dent bought the exclusive rights to Joanna but the face was not issued to the trade until 1958.

These three typefaces are from his most creative period, at Capel-y-ffin and his early years at Pigotts. At the same time he was working for Robert Gibbings' Golden Cockerell Press, including the typeface of that name and the typography and 'decorated letters' for the celebrated *Four Gospels.*

In 1935 Gill was made an Associate of the Institute of British Architects. Two years later he was made an Associate of the Royal Academy and in 1936, with J.H.MASON, was among the first group to be given the title Royal Designer for Industry. He died at home in 1940 after a lung operation.

SR/PB

Bertram Grosvenor GOODHUE 1869-1924 USA

Merrymount (1894)
Cheltenham (1896) **123**

A distinguished American architect whose best known buildings are the State Capital at Lincoln, Nebraska and the Church of St Thomas in New York, Bertram Grosvenor Goodhue has the even greater distinction of having created Cheltenham, one of the most successful American typefaces of the century.

Produced in 1896 by Ingalls Kimball of the Cheltenham Press in New York, 'Chelt' was probably the first typeface to be designed with the sole objective of achieving maximum legibility by the application of logical design principles: leading is an aid to legibility; ascenders are more important than descenders. It was also one of the first designs produced with the aid of the new pantographic punch-cutting, and was an immediate success. It was acquired by American Typefounders' in 1902 and has remained consistently popular for almost a century.

Goodhue designed Merrymount for the Merrymount Press, the private press run by D.B.Updike. Based on the JEN-SON letter, Merrymount shows the influence of William MOR-RIS and Updike regarded it as too black.

RCE

Fredric W.GOUDY   1865-1947   USA

Copperplate Gothic (1901) **236**
Pabst (1902) **468**
Powell (1903)
the first Village Type (1903)
Kennerley (1911) **6**
Forum Capitals (1912)
Goudy Antique/Lanston (1912)
Goudy Old Style (1915) **37**
GoudyType (1916)
Goudy Modern (1918) **132**
Goudy Open (1918)
Hadriano (1918)
Goudy Antique (1919)
Garamont (1921)
Newstyle (1921, adapted by Bruce Rogers 1945-46)
Frenchwood Ronde/Italian Old Style (1924) **32**
Goudy Extra Bold (1926)
Cushing Antique (1927) **101**
Goudy Text & Lombardic Capitals (1928)
Deepdene (1929-34) **21**
Kaatskill (1929)
Goudy Sans Serif (1930-31)
Mediæval (1930)
Goudy Village (1936)
Californian (1938)
Goudy Thirty (1946)

Frederic Goudy, was one of the best known and most prolific of type designers, by his own reckoning he designed 123 faces, (though he counts each italic as a separate face). Perhaps as a result, his output was uneven in quality.

Goudy was born in Bloomington Illinois in 1865 and was interested in type from an early age. He held several jobs in various cities before founding a printing business, the Booklet Press, in Chicago in 1895, with equipment bought from Will Bradley. Renamed the Camelot Press he printed the journal *American Chap-Book* before selling his interest a year later. His success in selling a set of capitals of his own design to the Bruce Type Foundry in Boston encouraged him to become a freelance lettering artist. He taught lettering and design at the Holme School of Illustration and developed an interest in the books and typography of the English private press movement. The Village Press was started in partnership with Will RANSOM, in 1903. It moved to Hingham, Mass., before going to New York in 1906. When the workshops were destroyed by fire in 1908 Goudy returned to his work as a lettering artist and designer. The following year he was able to visit Europe.

His breakthrough with type design came in 1911. He designed Kennerley Old Style for the publishers Mitchell Kennerley on the understanding that he could sell the type to the trade to recoup his costs. He set up the Village Letter Foundry to cast and sell Kennerley and a titling font, Forum. These established his reputation and were particularly popular in England. AMERICAN TYPEFOUNDERS' commissioned him to design a face for them and the result was Goudy Old Style, regarded by many critics as one of his finest designs. In 1920, with 40 types to his name Lanston MONOTYPE appointed Goudy as Art Advisor and it was in this capacity he worked on the revival Garamont.

The Village Press and letter foundry moved to Deepdene in New York State in 1925. In that same year, Robert Wiebking, who had made the matrices for most of his previous types, died. Although over 60, Goudy decided to learn about the practical aspects of type-founding and in the 12 years until his second workshop fire in 1939 he designed 60 typefaces.

Because of the number of his typefaces, many of Goudy's designs are variations on a theme. His best types however, in terms of critical appraisal as well as popularity,—Goudy Old Style and Goudy Text—are among the best examples of their kind.

Goudy also wrote about type, and surveyed the origins of his own designs in, *A half century of type design and typography 1895-1945*, written when he was nearly 80. Goudy died at his home, a watermill on the Hudson River in 1947.

SR

Philippe GRANDJEAN   1666-1714   F

Romains du Roi (1702)

The Romains du Roi is a significant development in the history of typography because it was the first real departure from the old style faces in use in Europe at the time, and as such can be considered the first transitional typeface.

Philippe Grandjean de Fouchy was born into an old Macon family in 1666, and is among those creators of typefaces said to owe their interest in type to a chance visit to a foundry or printers. A visit to a printing office in Paris led the young Grandjean to design a set of capitals. A Monsieur de Ponchartin, who was shown his early attempts, recommended him to Louis XIV and Grandjean was summoned to start working for the Imprimerie Royal under its director Jean Anisson. Later Granjean was to run the foundry and change its location as he moved house so it was always close to his home.

In 1692 Louis XIV appointed a committee from the Acadamie des Sciences to draw up plans for a new typeface which would be the exclusive property of the Imprimerie Royal. The committee, headed by Nicolas Jaugeon, studied types then in current use, historical manuscripts and principles of geometry. The letter designs it then drew up were based on divisions of the circle. The type was to be called the Romains du Roi, The King's Roman.

Grandjean was assigned to cut the new type and while guided by the drawings he did not follow them slavishly. The type established his reputation. He worked on it from 1694 to 1702. It appeared in its first size in 1702 in *Medailles sur le principaux événements du règne de Louis le Grand*. It was finally completed—in 21 sizes of roman and italic—in 1745. Jean Alexandre, Grandjean's assistant, took over the task of cutting it and was succeeded in turn by Louis Luce who also designed types in his own right.

As an attempt to protect the Romains du Roi from copying one letter was given a distinctive mark. It was reputedly Louis XIV who decided that this letter should be his initial: 'l'. In the lower case, the l has a little projection on the left hand side (a feature taken from a calligraphic l). In practice the Romains du Roi was copied anyway, sometimes with this special l, sometimes with the projection removed.

The design of the Romains du Roi is a step towards the modern face because it has shading which is closer to the vertical that on an old face type and also intensified contrast between the thick and the thin strokes. Its serifs are flat and unbracketed but not hairline (though it is unlikely that printing technology could have reproduced a hairline serif anyway at this time). Grandjean's italic also differs from the italic of the old face types. He regularised the slope and modified some of the letters.

The Romains du Roi continued to be used throughout the eighteenth century and despite being protected by law it was much copied (notably by P.S.FOURNIER and P.F.DIDOT).

SR

Robert GRANJON   active 1545-88 F

Civilité (1557)
[Granjon (1924, see GARAMOND & JONES*)]* **66**

Robert Granjon, like his father, began his career as a printer
in Paris as a partner to Michel Fezendat in 1549. Granjon
began supplying types around the same time, moved to Lyon
in 1557; later to Antwerp and finally to Rome where his
clients included the New Vatican Press. Nothing is known of
him after 1588.

Granjon designed and cut a great many types but he is best
known for his italics and for the script type which he called
the 'lettres Françaises' but which acquired the name Civilité
through its use in books of manners such as *Civilité puérile*.
Henri II granted a ten-year monopoly on the type to Granjon,
who printed twenty books which used it, but on the expiry of
the monopoly the type was not taken up by others in the way
its creator had hoped. Granjon had designed Civilité as a rival
to italic—a truly French one since it was based on current
French handwriting—but italic was too well established for
Civilité to be a threat. The type did prove more popular in Holland, and a Dutch version was created. In France it continued
to be used occasionally until the mid-eighteenth century

Robert Granjon's types were adopted enthusiastically by
other European printers of the day, most notably Christopher
PLANTIN, and in this century have provided the basis for
Plantin, Times New Roman and Galliard.

Granjon, the face that was named after him in G.W.
Jones's 1924 Linotype revival, was subsequently found to have
been based on a GARAMOND type.

SR

Chauncey H.GRIFFITH   1879-1956   USA

Ionic (1925) **121**
Poster Bodoni (1929) **440**
Excelsior (1931) **115**
Paragon (1935) **144**
Opticon (1935-6)
Janson (1937) **109**
Bell Gothic (1938) **285**
Corona (1941) **120**
Monticello (1946) **68**

In his position as Vice-President of Typographic Development for the Mergenthaler Linotype Company of New York, Chauncey H.Griffith was responsible for instigating many new designs, of which the best known is the Legibility Group: Ionic, Excelsior, Paragon, Opticon and Corona, all designed for the rigours of newspaper printing.

Griffith started his career as a journeyman compositor and pressman. When he joined Mergenthaler Linotype in 1906 it was as part of their sales force. He was made Sales Manager and Assistant to the President before taking charge of the company's typographical development programme. Two designers who worked for him were W.A. DWIGGINS and Rudolph RUZICKA. During his period with the company it issued revivals of Granjon, Baskerville, and Janson, a large number of Oriental scripts and helped prepare Bell Gothic for the Bell Telephone Company. The Legibility Group was begun in 1922 with Ionic, which was first used by the *Newark Evening News* in 1926. Excelsior, the second in the series, has been described as one of the most influential newspaper typefaces of all time.

During World War II he developed types to meet the US Government's desire that information in every dialect between California and the Chinese coast could be set using Linotype. His own favourite face was Monticello; based on the 1812 typeface Oxford, it was produced for setting *The Papers of Thomas Jefferson.*

Griffith retired from his position in 1949 but continued to work for Linotype as a consultant.

SR

Francesco GRIFFO, see MANUTIUS

André GÜRTLER   b.1936   CH

Basilia (1978) **152**
Unica (with C.Mengelt and E.Gschwind, 1980)

A recognized world authority on type and type design, André Gürtler is also a partner in Team 77 with Erich Gschwind and Christian Mengelt and is a member of the editorial panel of *Typographische Monatsblätter,* to which he has also contributed many articles.

Born in Switzerland, André Gürtler worked in the type

design drawing office of Monotype Corporation in England
and later as a designer at the Deberny & Peignot foundry in
France before joining the studio of Adrian Frutiger. He is currently a lecturer at the Basel School of Design where since
1965 he has lectured on the history and design of letterforms.

The typeface Unica, released by Haas, is a monoline sans
serif and combines features from Akzidenz Grotesk, Helvetica and Univers.

RCE

Johann GUTENBERG   c.1394–1468   D

Mainz Indulgence type (1455)
42-line Bible type (1455)

& Johann FUST & Peter SCHOEFFER

Mainz Psalter type (1457)
Durandus type (1459)
1462 Bible type

The German, Johann Gensfleisch zur Laden, known as Gutenberg, is generally believed to be the inventor of moveable
metal type, although there are some who credit the invention
to Laurents Coster of Haarlem. The invention, which probably
took place between 1440 and 1450, would have involved
Gutenberg's bringing together several existing techniques:
the screw press, oil-based pigments, the metal-working skills
of punch-cutting (which had been developed for patterning
metal), and casting. He was not a typographical innovator in
the sense of designing a new style of character. Rather than
modifying letter forms for print, he did his best to imitate the
lettering of books produced by contemporary scribes.

Gutenberg was born in Mainz where his father, Friele, was
a worker in precious metals, having connections with the
episcopal mint there. In 1428 Gutenberg left Mainz for Strasburg, where, although little is known of his life, we can
assume that he began work on the invention, for there are
records of his borrowing large sums of money and of pur-
chases of lead, a press and type.

He left Strasburg, probably in 1444 and is next heard of in
Mainz in 1448, where a year later he borrowed 800 guilders
for 'work on the books' from Johann Fust, a lawyer. A further
loan of 800 guilders proved necessary however, and at this
point Fust became a partner in the proceedings.

The principle works of Gutenberg's Mainz press were the

42-line Bible, probably completed in 1455—produced in two volumes of 324 and 318 pages respectively, which gets its name from the number of lines to a page—and the *Mainz Indulgences* of 1454-55. The Bible used type in the style of the German scribes of his day—textura—while the Indulgences used textura for headings, but a more open, almost cursive script—sometimes referred to as bastarda—for the text. The textura typeface used in the 42- *Line Bible* was later the inspiration for GOUDY's Goudy Text.

At some time during 1455 Fust, rather than risk simply being paid off, chose to foreclose on Gutenberg and continued the printing business with the aid of Peter Schoeffer, Gutenberg's foreman. Among the books they produced, using types which must have been essentially Gutenberg's work, were the *Mainz Psalters*, of 1457 and 1459, the *Rationale of Durandus*, and the *1462 Bible*.

Mainz became a centre for European printing where others, like Nicolas Jenson, went to learn the trade.

After the loss of his type, presses and money, little is known of Gutenberg's final years but his invention remained unchanged in its essentials until the industrial revolution and was the first real step in the movement towards universal literacy.

SR

HAAS'sche Schriftgiesserei AG   CH

The Swiss typefoundry Haas of Münchenstein had its origins in a printing works, with typefoundry attached, started in Basle in 1579, and is therefore the oldest typefoundry in the world. From 1740 the foundry, by now a separate business, came under the management of the Haas family who came from Nuremberg. Wilhelm Haas the elder (1741-1800) was the most important early figure in this family. A mathematician and a pioneer in punch-cutting who had been trained by Daniel Bernoulli, he first distinguished himself by constructing the world's first iron press and later went on to reform the typometric system.

In its early days the foundry had no typefaces of its own and it was not until about 1800 that the company, then under the direction of Wilhelm Haas the younger (1766-1838), began its first great era of creativity. During the following years the foundry became famous for its roman, italic, Gothic and schwarbacher typefaces. A special interest of Haas the younger was the cutting of foreign typefaces and by 1830 the foundry could boast that it could publish the Lord's Prayer in 100 different languages and dialects.

At the beginning of the twentieth century the foundry achieved international recognition for cutting some of the famous typefaces from earlier centuries, including Caslon and Bodoni. But the next great period of creativity came with the directors Eduard and Alfred Hoffmann who were committed to the creation of new typefaces by working in collaboration with leading graphic designers of the day. One of these was Max Miedinger, an in-house designer with Haas, who designed Helvetica in 1956. Helvetica went on to become one of the most widely used sans serif typefaces. Other designers at this time included Edmund Thiele and Walter DIETHELM.

In more recent times the range of typefaces offered by Haas has been greatly extended by the acquisition of a number of other famous typefoundries, notably DEBERNY & PEIGNOT in 1972, Fonderie Olive and the typefounding department of BERTHOLD & Stempel. Today the range of typefaces in the company's catalogue numbers over 200.

RCE

Victor HAMMER   1882-1967   AU

Hammer Unziale (1921)
Pindar (1933-35)
American Uncial (1943)
Andromaque Uncial (1958) **377**
Samson

Victor Hammer was a distinguished printer who devoted a great deal of his life to the design and development of the letter form known as the uncial, the writing hand used by mediæval scribes between the fourth and ninth centuries. He used his uncial designs to print all his books, which were invariably printed on a hand press and were greatly admired. His aim was to achieve a letter form which would unify the roman and black-letter traditions.

An Austrian, Victor Hammer was a prominent portraitist and sculptor in Vienna who, in his youth, had been inspired by the work and ideals of William MORRIS, from whom his interest in typography and printing probably sprang. His first uncial type design was cut in 1921 by A.Schuricht and was later produced by the Klingspor foundry at Offenbach under the name Hammer Unziale. Although commercially success-ful, Hammer was not satisfied with this face and resolved to learn the art of punch-cutting himself.

Meanwhile he set up his first printing press in Florence, Italy, and in 1929 he moved the press to the Villa Santuccio and called it Stamperia del Santuccio, which became the imprint on all his books. His first book was Milton's SAMSON AGONISTES for which he created his second uncial, Samson, cut by Rudolf KOCH's son, Paul. His next uncial, Pindar, was the first type cut by his own hand—without, it is claimed—any attempt at first drawing the letters.

In 1939 he fled the Nazis, leaving all his cutting and cast-ing tools in Austria, and most of his fonts, and went to the USA where he had been offered a post teaching art and let-tering at Wells College in New York. It was here that he start-ed work on American Uncial, his best known type and for which he cut the steel punches by hand. With the help of the Society of Typographic Arts in Chicago and R.H.MIDDLETON, sufficient money was raised to complete the project but the face was not produced commercially until after the war when Klingspor produced it for sale in Europe and the USA.

His last uncial was called Andromaque (after the Greek legend). Cut by the French typefounders Deberny & Peignot in 1958, Andromaque resembles Greek cursive letters and shows no evidence of the predominantly mediæval character associ-ated with all his other types. Originally cut in 10pt, a 14pt ver-sion of Andromaque was started but not completed at the time of his death in 1967. The cutting was completed howev-er, by R.H.Hunter in collaboration with Hammer's widow, Carolyn Reading Hammer.

Hammer's single-minded approach to type design was unusual and highly idiosyncratic; his various attempts at the uncial form stretched over a period of more than forty years and were an inspiration to many other leading figures of his generation who went on to experiment with the uncial form. Among them F.W.GOUDY (Friar), S.H.DE ROOS (Libra), and G.G.LANGE (Solemnis).

RCE

ꝛuaíꞃíoh maclennan

Victor Hammer's American Uncial

Sem L.HARTZ   b.1912   NL

Emergo (1948-53)
Juliana (1958)
Molé Foliate (1960) **544**

Sem L. Hartz was well known as an engraver of stamp and
banknote designs before he began designing and cutting
types to keep himself busy during the German occupation of
the Netherlands during the World War II.

He was born in Leyden, where his father, the painter Louis
Hartz, taught him art. He continued his education at the
Academy of Fine Arts in Amsterdam where he specialised in
copper engraving and joined Joh. Enschedé en Zonen in Haarlem as an apprentice, eventually succeeding Jan VAN KRIMPEN
as cheif designer. Although hand punch-cutting had by then
almost died out, he cut his first typeface Emergo by hand onto
steel punches without doing finished drawings first. A book
type, Emergo, was produced by Enschedé, and after the liber-
ation Hartz used it for his own private press. His next type,
Juliana, also a book type, was commissioned by Linotype and
being fairly narrow, it proved quite popular in England for
paperbacks. Molé Foliate is a redrawing of an 1819 design by
the Paris founder Molé-le-Jeune.

Hartz's other work includes glass-engraving and book
illustration. An exhibition of his work was held in The Hague
in 1969.

SR

Michael HARVEY   b.1931   GB

Grot R (1964)
Zephyr (1964)
Stamford (1966)
Millbank (1982)
Ellington (1990)

Michael Harvey, who describes himself as 'letterer and jazz-
lover', has designed 1,500 book-jackets for Methuen, Cambrige University Press, The Bodley Head, and others. His
designs are always lettering designs, and have rarely included
illustrations.

He was working as an engineering draughtsman when,
aged 20, he read Eric GILL's autobiography. He spent two periods with Joseph Cribb, Gill's first apprentice, before working

Among Michael Harvey's largest stone-carving commissions was for the Sainsbury Wing of the National Gallery in London which opened in 1991.   (Photo: Michael Harvey)

for Reynolds STONE for six years where one of his first jobs was carving inscriptions on the slate panels for the tomb of Duff Cooper, the writer and politician.

He began working freelance in 1961 and has combined this with teaching and writing. His books include *Lettering design, Creative lettering: drawing and design, Carving letters in stone & wood* and *Calligraphy in the graphic arts.*

Michael Harvey has designed several display faces; Grot R and Stamford for the exclusive use of the The Bodley Head, Millbank for the Tate Gallery, and Zephyr, which was cut by the Ludlow Typefoundry. His text typeface Ellington was designed for MONOTYPE and named after the famous jazz musician, Duke Ellington.

RCE

Ashley HAVINDEN   1903-73   GB

Ashley Crawford (1930)
Ashley Script (1955) **357**

Ashley Havinden was director and art director at W.S.Crawford, the London advertising agency, and also a director of the associated industrial design company, Sir William Crawford & Partners. He was one of the best-known figures in the advertising world in the periods immediately preceding and following World War II. He was appointed Royal Designer in Industry and was awarded an OBE in 1951 for services to industrial design.

RCE

Sol HESS 1886-1953 USA

Bruce Old Style No.31 (1909) **173**
Tourist Gothic (1909)
Hess Bold (1910)
Hess Old Style (1920-23)
Stymie (1931) **199, 200**
Hess Neobold (1933) **461**
Spire (1938)
Squareface (1939)
Artscript (1940)
Sans Serif Extra Bold, ~Extra Bold Condensed, ~Medium Condensed, ~Lined
Twentieth Century

For fifty years Sol Hess was art director of Lanston MONOTYPE Machinery Co. where he succeeded his friend and collaborator W.F.GOUDY. He started with the company in 1902 after a three-year scholarship course at Pennsylvania Museum School of Industrial Art, and as a type designer there he redrew and readapted all their typographical materials. His forte was the development of type families and during his years with Lanston Monotype he carried out commissions for many leading American companies, including Curtis Publishing, Crowell-Collier, Sears Roebuck, Montgomery Ward, Yale University Press and World Publishing Company.

RCE

Cynthia HOLLANDSWORTH b.1955 USA

Hiroshige (1986)
Tiepolo (1987)
Wile Roman (1990)

Cynthia Hollandsworth is the Manager of Type Design and Development at Agfa COMPUGRAPHIC in Massachusetts, and a typeface designer who has released a number of typefaces through her company, AlphaOmega Typography. She is also an advisor to the ITC Typeface Review Board.

In 1987 she formed the Typeface Design Coalition to work for legal protection of typeface design and software in the United States. Members of the coalition include Agfa Compugraphic, MONOTYPE, LINOTYPE, ITC, Hewlett-Packard, BITSTREAM, ADOBE and many others.

A major project which she is currently undertaking, in cooperation with Barbara Gibb, is the reworking of the Schneidler typeface created for the BAUER foundry in the 30s but not issued because of the outbreak of World War II. When completed it will be issued by Bauer as Schneidler Antiqua.

RCE

Kris HOLMES b.1950 USA

Shannon (1982, with Janice Prescott)
Isadora (1985)
Lucida (1985, with Charles BIGELOW)
Sierra (1989)

Kris Holmes is a partner in the design studio of Bigelow & Holmes. She was born in California and studied calligraphy with Lloyd Reynolds and Robert Palladino at Reed College in Oregon and later went on to obtain a Bachelor of Arts degree from Harvard University.

With her partner, Charles BIGELOW, she created Lucida, an extended family of serif, sans serif, Greek, scientific and linguistic alphabets designed for laser printing which have been adopted by the journal *Scientific American.* She has designed several revival typefaces for Rudolf Hell (now part of Linotype), and her lettering and calligraphy have appeared in many publications, such as *Fine Print* and *International Calligraphy Today.*

Along the way she also studied modern dance at the Martha Graham School in New York.

RCE

ITC (International Typeface Corporation) USA

ITC was founded in 1969 and although it is the world's major institutional supplier of typefaces it does not follow the normal pattern of type founders. In fact, ITC has no manufacturing facilities and is really a marketing organisation supplying typeface designs to facility houses.

The chief marketing tool for the company's products is the

house magazine *U&lc* which has a circulation of over 200,000 and a readership of many times that. Directed primarily at end-users of type rather than the facility houses or system manufacturers, *U&lc* is a highly effective shop window for new typefaces. In its early years the use of innovative design and imaginative typography earned it a reputation as a fore-runner of style.

The concept of ITC had its origins in the partnership of Herb LUBALIN and Aaron Burns (1922-91) working in coopera-tion with Edward Rondthaler, who at that time was operating a New York photolettering house. Herb Lubalin became the first editor of *U&lc*, a position for which he was uniquely qualified and which he held until his death in 1981. Many of the early faces for ITC were designed by Herb Lubalin and Ed BENGUIAT and were influenced by the taste of the New York advertising industry, but later designs showed a broader approach and included many more restrained text faces.

Typeface designs at ITC are selected from submissions by type designers throughout the world and after a careful review procedure four typeface families are issued each year. ITC also commissions typefaces from internationally known type designers. Matthew CARTER, Herman ZAPF and many other designers mentioned in this book have carried out com-missions for them. The company currently offers a library of over 400 typefaces.

International Typeface Corporation was acquired by Esselte LETRASET in 1986 but the company still operates inde-pendently from their offices in New York.

RCE

Joseph JACKSON 1733-92 GB

Joseph Jackson, although not an innovator in terms of type design, was acknowledged to be one of the most skillful punch-cutters of his generation. He was born in Old Street, London, and was an apprentice at the foundry of William CASLON in Chiswell Street. Jackson, although willing and capable in most aspects of the business, received no instruc-tion in punch-cutting. The art of punch-cutting was carried out in secret at the Chiswell Street foundry so Jackson bored a hole in the wainscot of an adjoining room and took to spy-ing on William Caslon and his son. In good time he mastered the secrets of the art and prepared his first punch which, unwisely perhaps, he showed to his master, who promptly boxed his ears and told him never to do it again.

But do it again he did: this time at home with tools bought by his mother, and eventually he became very good at it. So good in fact, that when he and a colleague called Thomas Cottrell were discharged by Caslon because of a dispute about wages, the two joined forces and set up in business. Jackson, on the death of his mother in 1759, joined the Navy as an armourer (Caslon had started as a gun engraver) and did not return to typefounding until the peace of 1763 when, with prizemoney of £40 in his pocket, he rejoined his old colleague Cottrell who now had a foundry in Fetter Lane.

For a time Jackson worked for Cottrell for an annual salary of £62/8/-, but eventually set up his own business in a small house in Cock Lane before moving to larger premises in Salisbury Square near Fleet Street. Because of his undoubted skill as a punch-cutter the business made rapid progress and William Caslon and his son both acknowledged his supreme craftsmanship. In 1767 he was commissioned to cut a facsimile type for the *Domesday Book* and later he was asked to cut the type for Waid's facsimile of the *New Testament of the Alexandrian Codex* in the British Museum. When the latter was printed in 1786 Jackson, now famous, was paid the unusual honour of a credit on the title page.

A more difficult task was the brilliantly executed type cut for Kipling's facsimile edition of the *Codex Bezae*. The most important works of his later years were the type for Macklin's Bible, to which Vincent Figgins later contributed, and a type prepared for a sumptuous edition of Hume's *History of England*. Unfortunately, neither works appeared until after his death.

In 1790 the foundry was seriously damaged by a fire in which many moulds and matrices were lost or destroyed and the shock of this seriously affected his health and his ability to work. But he was unusually fortunate in that his assistant was Vincent FIGGINS who had started with him as an apprentice in 1782 and who was later to become one of the greatest typefounders of the age. Figgins was more than capable of managing the foundry and did so until Jackson's death from scarlet fever in 1792. After Jackson's death Figgins was not in a financial position to purchase the business and it was sold to William Caslon III who had recently disposed of his interest in the family foundry at Chiswell Street by selling his share to his mother and sister-in-law

RCE

Jean JANNON   1580-1658   F

Caractères de l'Université (1621)
Garamond/Garamont/Garaldus (1912/1930/1956, see
Jannon/Goudy/Novarese) **91-95/96**

The Frenchman Jean Jannon was a printer and punch-cutter
to the Protestant academy at Sedan, where his types, now
known as the Caractères de l'Université were confiscated at
the order of Cardinal Richelieu and were later placed in the
care of the Imprimerie Royale—French Royal Printing Office—
which the cardinal had established in 1640.

Although based very much on Garamond's types, Jannon
refined some of the features, particularly the angle of the serifs of s, m, n, p, and r.

They were used for the 1642 edition of Cardinal Richelieu's memoirs but thereafter were forgotten until 1825 when
they were rediscovered and attributed to Garamond. In the
early years of this century they were used as the basis for the
many Garamond revivals then being issued, and it was not
until 1925 that Monotype's Beatrice Warde proved that they
were in fact by Jean Jannon with the discovery of his 1621
specimen sheet.

SR

Nicolas JENSON   1420-80   F

Jenson (see Phinney) **16**

Nicolas Jenson was one of the first printers to use type based
on the model of the traditional roman letter, rather than the
dark gothic type used in earlier German printed books.

Although known for his work in Venice, Jenson was a
Frenchman, born in Sommevoire in the district of Cham-
pagne around 1420. He served an apprenticeship in the Paris
mint and was promoted to be Master of the Mint at Tours.
Apparently Charles VII sent Jenson to Mainz in 1458 in order
that he should discover more about the new invention of
printing, but from 1470 until his death he worked in Venice,
first as his own master, and, after the slump of 1473, as head
of a syndicate. His roman type was first used in Eusebius' *De
Praeparatio Evangelica* in 1470 and was one of the first to be
designed conscientiously according to typographic ideals and
in rejection to manuscript models.

Although he never printed a Greek book (most of his work

was Latin classics) he was the first Venetian printer to produce Greek characters for use with other texts. Previously Greek words would be written in by hand.

He continued to publish regularly until his death in September 1480. Around 155 editions exist known to be printed by Jenson or attributed to his press. Pope Sixtus IX made him Count Palantine, probably as a reward for publishing devotional works.

He was involved in several partnerships with other Venetian printers. The company of John of Cologne & Nicolas Jenson is mentioned in his will, made shortly before his death. It continued to print until John of Cologne died five years later. In the will Jenson left his punches to another partner, Peter Ugelheimer.

Jenson's roman had a great influence when a revival of interest in printing and typography took place in the late nineteenth and early twentieth centuries. Among the faces that took his as a model were MORRIS's Golden (1890), the Doves Press roman of COBDEN-SANDERSON (1899) and Bruce ROGER's Montaigne (1902).

SR

Edward JOHNSTON   1872-1944   GB

Cranach Press Italic
Johnston/London Underground Type (1916)

Edward Johnston was a central figure in the Arts & Crafts movement at the turn of the century and was instrumental in the revival of the art of calligraphy in England and Germany in the first thirty years of this century. Among those who were inspired by him was Eric GILL.

Edward Johnston studied medicine in Edinburgh before coming to London to study art. A discovery of the manuscripts in the British Library led to a lifelong addiction to lettering. He approached W.R.Lethaby to join a lettering class at the Central School of Arts & Crafts but instead was appointed to take the calligraphy class which he began in 1899. Johnston was aware of MORRIS's study of roman letters and built on this, he was more systematic and his classes were both practical and inspirational.

Eric Gill joined the class in 1901 and it was the start of a long friendship between the two men. Gill shared rooms with Johnston for a while at Lincoln's Inn, and from 1905 they were near neighbours in Hammersmith, centre of the original Arts & Crafts movement and home at various times to the Chiswick Press, Morris's Kelmscott Press and WALKER & COB-DEN-SANDERSON's Doves Press. In 1906 Johnston published what is now regarded as the most influential calligraphy book ever written, *Writing & Illuminating, & Lettering.* It had taken him three and a half years to write and Eric Gill contributed a chapter entitled *Inscriptions in stone.* Other notable pupils of Johnston's include the type designer Ernst F.DETTERER and the designer Anna Simons whose German translation of *Writing & Illuminating, & Lettering* found a new and responsive audience for his ideas.

Johnston is responsible for the first of the modern chancery italics. Designed for Count Harry Kessler's Cranach Press and called Cranach Press Italic this type was based on the type of a Venetian scribe, Tagliente, which appeared in a writing book of 1524. This italic was to accompany a roman created for Kessler by Emery Walker, the draughtsman Percy Tiffin and punch-cutter Edward Prince (Tiffin and Prince also worked on Johnston's italic).

Johnston was one of the founder/editors of the highly influential journal *The Imprint* which came out for just nine issues in 1913. The others were Gerard Meynell, John H.MASON and F.Ernst Jackson, and with them he had an influence on the typeface Imprint. Meynell is said to have recommended his work to Frank Pick of London Transport and in 1915 Johnston was commissioned by Pick to design what has become his best known face.

Johnston was designed for the exclusive use of London Underground to provide them with one consistent style for all their signs and notices. Johnston produced a sans serif face based on classical Roman forms rather than on the nineteenth-century grotesques. Eric Gill helped Johnston in the early stages of the work and received 10% of the fee. Later, around 1927, he was to use similar forms for his Gill Sans.

Johnston was working for London Transport as late as 1933 and continued to work until about 1940 when he was forced to stop because of illness, it is hard to overestimate his influence; later, remembering his time as a pupil, Gill reported being 'struck as by lightning', he was not alone.

SR

George William JONES   1860-1942   GB

Granjon (1928-31) **66**
Venezia (1928, italic by F.W.GOUDY*)*
Estienne (1930)

George W.Jones was a renowned printer with a keen interest
in early printing and typography and a fine library of books.
He placed great emphasis on quality and was at the forefront
of what became known as the 'Renaissance of printing' in the
late nineteenth and early twentieth centuries. His printing
company, based in Gough Square in London, was called the
Sign of the Dolphin.

English LINOTYPE made Jones their printing adviser in
1921 to help them plan a series of type revivals. They were the
first British company to create such a position (MONOTYPE
were to follow with the appointment of Stanley MORISON).

Jones designed Granjon as a rival to Monotype Garamond,
taking as his model a font of type used by the Paris printers
Jacques Dupuys & Jean Poupy and named it in honour of
Robert GRANJON, the sixteenth century punch-cutter. These
types were later proved by Beatrice Warde to have been GARA-
MOND's while the Garamond revivals were shown to have
been based on types by Jean JANNON. Estienne, which takes its
name from a famous Paris printing family, is also based on
French types from that period. Venezia was originally cut for
the Sign of the Dolphin by Edward PRINCE, an italic was added
by Frederic Goudy in 1925 and it was subsequently issued by
Monotype.

Jones lectured on letterpress in Britain and the United
States. At 28 he helped found the journal *British Printer* and
was a founder of The British Typographia, an association for
the advancement of education in printing. His work was
much praised; Henry Lewis Bullen called him 'the best all-
round printer that Great Britain has ever produced.'

SR

Heinrich JOST   1889-1948   D

Fraktur (1925) **366**
Atrax (1926)
Bauer Bodoni (1926) **153**
Jost Mediæval/Aeterna (1927)
Beton (1931-36) **189**

Heinrich Jost was best known as the art director of the BAUER type foundry in Frankfurt but he also designed Fraktur for Monotype and Jost Mediæval for Ludwig & Mayer (Mediæval, in German typography, roughly equates with our Venetian).

Jost was the son of a bookbinder, but started his own career selling books and later studied book production in Paul RENNER's Advanced School of German Bookprinting in Munich. After leaving he worked for a daily paper and various Munich publishers before being invited to Bauer by George Hartmann. Beton, Bauer Bodoni and Atrax were created for Bauer, with Beton quickly establishing itself as a popular advertising face. Bauer Bodoni is the rival to M.F.BENTON's ATF Bodoni, which was the model for most other versions. Bauer Bodoni is closer in feeling to the original, the serifs are very delicately bracketted while the transition from thick to thin is not as severe as Benton's. It is one of a number of revivals cut by the foundry.

Jost also commissioned faces from artists and teachers of typography, and at the time of his death he was working on a survey of typographers.

SR

Albert KAPR   b.1918   D

Faust (1959)
Leipzig (1963)

Albert Kapr has designed seven typefaces, including Faust and Leipzig, and has written many books on design and typography. He has won many awards for book design and the Gutenberg prize. He lives in Leipzig.

Born in Stuttgart, Albert Kapr started as an apprentice compositor but his apprenticeship was interrupted by spells in concentration camp and prison. Later, with an intermission of five years service in the army, he completed his studies at the Stuttgarter Akademie from 1938 to 1948.

He was appointed lecturer at the Academy of Fine Arts in Weimar, and in 1951 he became Professor at the Hochschule für Graphic und Buchkunst in Leipzig where, from 1956 to 1978, he was head of the Institute of Book Design. He was elected Rector of the Hochschule in 1959, and again from 1966 to 1973. From 1964 to 1977 he was art director for the Typoart typefoundry in Dresden, for whom he designed two typefaces.

RCE

David Kindersley's MOT Serif. (Photo: David Kindersley)

David **KINDERSLEY** **b.1915** GB

MOT Serif, motorway alphabet (c.1961)
Octavian (with Will CARTER, 1961) **234**
Kindersley, street name alphabet (c.1962)
Itek Bookface (1976)

A great reviver and champion of the serif letter and a follow-
er of Eric Gill, David Kindersley was born in Codicote, Hert-
fordshire. He was educated at St. Cyprians and Marlborough,
after which he was sent to Paris to study French. It was here
that he met Britten Rivière with whom he studied sculpture,

mainly modelling in clay. But the young Kindersley was soon attracted to working in stone, a passion which has remained with him throughout his life, and the skill for which he is best known today.

After a short period of working in stone work with the Induni brothers he returned to England where he was immediately attracted by the work of Eric GILL, and at the age of eighteen he persuaded Gill to take him on as an apprentice. As with so many, Gill had a profound influence on the eager and talented young student and Kindersley continued in the Gill studio until 1939 when, at the age of 21, he set up his own workshop in Cambridge.

Although a reluctant teacher he was persuaded to take a class in Cambridge, where by a happy chance one of his students was Will Carter, with whom Kindersley later created for Monotype the typeface Octavian, his first serious effort in the field of type design. Also at Cambridge he met Brooke Crutchley, the university printer, which led to an important commission to produce lettering for the Cambridge University Press building.

A variety of commissions followed including alphabets for street signs, work on film titles for the Shell Film Unit and, in 1953, his most important project at that time, the lettering for the American War Cemetery near Cambridge.

One episode that typifies Kindersley's approach to the serif letter was the commission to produce a typeface for road signs. This was to be a competitive commission in which Kindersley's offering was to be compared with a sans serif typeface designed by KINNEIR/Calvert. A series of tests carried out by the Road Research Laboratory showed that in terms of recognition and legibility at speed, Kindersley's capitalized serif letters were greatly superior to the modernist sans serif, upper-and-lower-case letters. But despite this conclusive result the sans serif was chosen.

So much of Kindersley's work is dependent on the artist's hand and eye that he deliberately set about experimenting with electronic methods to recreate the subtle variation in letter spacing which until then could only be achieved by hand. His object was to find a system to improve the spacing of all forms of setting, particularly in text composition. The firm of Letraset, then still new, were greatly interested in this work and soon awarded him a consultancy which continued until 1986. This particular contribution to typesetting, although entirely logical today, was of immense significance when Kindersley first started it in the 50s.

David Kindersley stands apart from the mainstream of type designers. Like Gill Before him, and perhaps even more so, stone is his preferred medium, but this does not diminish his contribution; on the contrary, in an age of increasing mechanisation he still carries a torch for the master craftsman. His lovingly and painstakingly executed works in marble, stone, slate and wood are superb examples of the letterers' art, many of which may well survive the printed page. He was chairman of the Wynkyn de Worde Society in 1976.

RCE

KINGSLEY ATF,
see AMERICAN TYPEFOUNDERS'

Jock KINNEIR   b. 1917   GB
& Margaret CALVERT   b.1936   SA

Transport, road/rail alphabet, (c.1963) **282**
Calvert (1980) **190**

Kinneir & Calvert have designed lettering and signing systems that are used all over Britain and extensively outside it. Their first such project was in the mid-50s for Gatwick Airport and the last, in 1977, was for the Tyne & Wear Metro.

Jock Kinneir studied engraving at Chelsea College of Art, and later lectured there. He worked in the Design Research Unit of the Central Office of Information and in that capacity was involved in the design for the Festival of Britain. In 1945 he set up on his own and when he began the work for Gatwick Airport in 1958 he took on Margaret Calvert, one of his students, to help him. Margaret Calvert came to England in 1950 and attended St. Paul's School in London before going to Chelsea School of Art from 1954 to 1957 to study illustration. In 1964 she became a partner in Kinneir/Calvert Associates.

Following the Gatwick Airport lettering, they designed the sign system for the motorway system then under construction, and as a result Kinneir was appointed to the Warboys Committee on road signs.

They were one of the first British advocates of the idea that sans serif upper and lower-case letters are intrinsically more legible for signage systems, and despite the Road Research Laboratory test results of David KINDERSLEY's all upper-case, serif letter designs proving otherwise, the Kinneir/Calvert alphabet, Transport, was used, being introduced in 1964.

British Rail then commissioned signs using the same lettering for the national rail network and many other public bodies followed suit including the British Airports Authority, the National Health Service and the Army.

The typeface Calvert, an egyptian, grew out of a plan for lettering for Saint Quentin-en-Yveline. Though this French new town found the style too English it was used successfully on signs for the Tyne & Wear Metro in 1977. Calvert adapted it into a type by reducing it and then calculating the adjustments needed for the new weights and x-height. Monotype produced working drawings for her originals and the face was issued to the trade in 1980.

Jock Kinneir was head of the Department of Graphic Design at the Royal College of Art, London from 1964 to 1969 and continued to teach there until 1974. Margaret Calvert also teaches at the Royal College of Art and has been head of the Department of Graphic Arts & Design since 1987.

SR

Nicholas KIS   1650-1702   H

Janson (1937, see C.H.GRIFFITH*)* **109**
Ehrhardt (1938) **73**

Nicholas Kis was a Hungarian punch-cutter who worked in Amsterdam. His types are some of the greatest in the Dutch old face style and have been used as models for a number of developments in this century. The Linotype version of this style, Janson, was created by C.H.Griffith in 1937 and is based on an original face cut by Kis in 1670-90. The face is named after Anton Janson, a Dutchman who worked in Leipzig, with whom the face has no connection.

Ehrhardt, produced by Monotype in 1938, is another Dutch old face type similar to Janson and Van Dijck. It is based on a type cut by Kis in 1672 and the name derives from the fact that and the original types were held by the Ehrhardt foundry in Leipzig.

RCE

Typefoundry Gebruder KLINGSPOR   D

Founded in Offenbach in 1842 as the Typefoundry Johann Peter Nees & Co., and from 1859 known as Rudhardsche

Giesserie, it was bought by Carl Klingspoor in 1892 and managed by his sons, Karl and Wilhelm. By the turn of the century it was well known throughout Germany and in 1902 the architect Peter BEHRENS produced his typeface for the foundry.

In 1906 the name was changed to Typefoundry Gebruder (=Brothers) Klingspor, and in that same year Rudolph KOCH began to work for the foundry. He was to stay for the rest of his life, designing 28 typefaces for them including his celebrated sans serif, Kabel. During Koch's years at Offenbach, where he remained for the rest of his career, the chief outside designer was Walter TIEMANN, a co-founder, with Carl Ernst Poeschel, of the Janus Press, Germany's first private press.

Karl Klingspor died in 1950, and in 1956 the foundry was sold to D.Stempel AG of Frankfurt.

PB

Rudolf KOCH   1876-1934   D

Deutsche Schrift (1910)
Maximillian Antiqua (1914)
Koch Antiqua/Locano (1922) **569**
Neuland (1923)
Klingspor Schrift (1924-26)
Wallou (1925-30)
Wilhelm (1925)
Cable/Kabel **258,**
& variants ~Initials, Prisma & Zeppelin (1927-29)
Jessen (c.1926)
Marathon (1931)
Holla (1932)
Offenbach (1935)
Claudius (1937)
Steel/Stahl (with Hans Kuehne, 1939)

One of the most respected designers and teachers of his day, Rudolf Koch was first and foremost a calligrapher and all the types he designed, except one, were developed from calligraphy. Later in life he was to say,

> Lettering gives me the purest and greatest pleasure, and on
> countless occasions it has been to me what a song is to a singer...

Koch designed more than a score of faces for Klingspor and towards the end of his career he cut three himself.

Born in Nuremberg the son of a sculptor, Rudolf Koch experienced early misfortune when, in 1886, his father died, and as a result he was soon apprenticed in a metal foundry in Hanau. He attended evening classes at the Art School and left the foundry before completing his apprenticeship. Returning to Nuremburg he tried to train as a teacher and to sit examinations in art but the incompatibility of the Prussian and Bavarian education systems prevented this and in 1898 he found work as a designer in Leipzig.

It was the high time of Jungendstil—art nouveau—an exciting and confusing time for any artist of Koch's generation, and Koch became a devotee. At about this time he began experimenting with a broad-nibbed pen and found that he was able to master many calligraphic styles, and at last he felt that he was beginning to find his forte.

At the age of 30 he saw an advertisement in a trade magazine for the post of designer in a small firm of typefounders at Offenbach. The company was Rudhardsche Giesserei, later known as the Klingspor typefoundry. Koch, broadly experienced but with little else to his credit, applied for the job and was accepted. The relationship was to prove a long and fruitful one for Koch, the company and the future of type design in Germany.

Shortly after joining Klingspor, Koch designed his first typeface, Deutsche Schrift, a bold blackletter which occupied him until 1910. As with all his types, his method was to experiment with hand-drawn letters using a broad pen. The same letters would be drawn again and again until every letter was complete and perfect, and the type ready to be cut.

During World War I Koch was enlisted and sent to the battle fronts in Serbia and France. Discharged in 1918, he was a changed man. As a result he became even more deeply engrossed in his work, and the post-war years were to see the beginning of his most creative and productive period. First came Neuland then Wilhelm Klingspor Schrift, the summit of his achievement in a purely blackletter tradition. Jesson, which he cut himself, was a simplified blackletter with romanised capitals, created originally for the great edition of the *Four Gospels* printed by the Klingspor press in 1926.

With Kabel, Koch overcame his personal resistance to the sans serif letter. Designed at the same time as Paul Renner's more popular Futura, Kabel retains traditional roman forms for a, g, and t, and a venetian e. Some characters have oblique stroke endings, making it unique among sans serifs until Hans Meyer's Syntax of 1967.

By the mid 1920s, a man of some eminence, Koch had

founded the Offenbach Werkstatt, a small class of dedicated students consisting of Friedl Heinrichsen, Carl Vollmer, Fritz Kredel, Berthold WOLPE and Richard Bender, many of whom were to have an important role themselves in later years. Despite—or perhaps because of—the fact that circumstances had deprived him of a fine education it was a subject that he took very seriously. 'I am nothing but an educator', he is reported to have said on one occasion.

A deeply religious man, he combined in his character the single-mindedness of a hard, serious and conscientious worker, with the qualities of a warmhearted, loyal and helpful friend.   RCE

Volker KUSTER   b.1941   D

Today Sans Serif (1989)

Born in Wernigerode, East Germany, and apprenticed as a typesetter, Volker Kuster attended the Arts Trade School in Berlin from 1961 to 1964. He took further studies with Albert KAPR at Leipzig University where he later went on to tutor in typography and type design from 1969 to 1975. Throughout this period he undertook freelance design work in Leipzig and collaborated with Typoart in Dresden. He was Type Director for Scangraphic in Hamburg from 1984 to 1988 for whom he designed the Today Sans Serif family, an informal design with 40 variations.

RCE

Günther Gerhard LANGE   b.1921   D

Arena (1951-59)
Derby (1953)
Solemnis (1954)
Boulevard (1955)
Champion (1957)
El Greco (1964)
Concorde (1968-78) **100**
Imago (1982) **274**

Artistic Director of H.Berthold AG, Günther Gerhard Lange has been responsible for the company's entire typeface development programme since 1960. In addition to reviving several classic faces he has also created many new typefaces, including Concorde and Imago.

Born in Frankfurt in 1921 he studied calligraphy, type

design, drawing, etching and lithography at the Academie für Graphische Künst und Buchgewerbe in Leipzig from 1941 to 1945, where his tutors included George Belwe for calligraphy and typesetting and Hans Theo Richter for lithography. After a period as a freelance painter and graphic designer he moved to Berlin in 1949 and undertook further studies in painting and drawing at the Hochschule für Bildende Künste.

A calligraphic influence shows itself in some of his types. His early Derby and Boulevard are both script types, as are Champion and El Greco. His 1954 Solemnis is an uncial and was part of the revival of such forms begun by Victor HAM-MER. Arena is a roman body type which bears the influence of Stanley MORISON's Times.

His career with Berthold commenced in 1950 when he was employed as an artistic freelance. After his appointment as Artistic Director in 1960 he was appointed to the main board in 1971.

RCE

LETRASET (Esselte Letraset)   GB (CH)

Before the introduction of Letraset dry transfer lettering in 1961, the traditional method of preparing lettering for display and headline work was by hand—a time consuming and labour-intensive process involving the use of highly skilled artists and designers. Suddenly, commercial artists were able to produce accurate, high-quality lettering in a fraction of the time by transferring pre-printed lettering directly onto artwork. It is hardly surprising that designers, graphic artists, commercial artists, and many others, hailed it as a revolution in the studio.

Letraset Ltd was formed in 1959, but its origins go back to an idea of J.C.C.(Dai) Davies in 1956. He developed the technique with Fred McKenzie from a wet transfer system which had been in use for some time as a child's toy. Bob Chudley, who had worked for Crawford's, the London advertising agency, and also for leading London department stores—two areas in which the rapid production of display lettering was of paramount importance—saw the potential for the technique and steered the development in its early stages.

Once launched the product was an immediate success (helped by a printers strike in 1959) and the company went public in 1963, by which time a network of international distributors had been established in 70 countries. Such was the success of the venture that at the flotation of the company the shares were over-subscribed 140 times and the shares opened at a premium of 70% over their issue price. In the following year sales rose to £750,000 with 75% of the company's production going to export, an achievement which led to the Queen's Award for Export in 1966.

Today there are 750 typefaces available from the company, of which nearly half are exclusive to Letraset. Many of these faces have been designed in-house by Colin BRIGNALL, the company's type director since 1980.

In 1981, the company was acquired by Esselte, the Swiss-based international group, and Letraset changed its name to Esselte Letraset Limited. AMERICAN TYPEFOUNDERS' was acquired by Esselte Letraset in 1986 and operates as a separate company from New York.

As typesetting systems have become cheaper and more flexible however, the advantages of dry-transfer lettering have diminished. Letraset has responded by diversifying into software programs for use on the Macintosh. These include LetraStudio, a headline type manipulation program; and FontStudio, a type designing program for creating PostScript format fonts.

RCE

Zuzana LICKO b.1961 CS
& EMIGRÉ FONTS USA

Oakland (1986)
Emigré (1986)
Emperor (1986)
Matrix (1986)
Modula Sans (1986)
Universal (1986)
Modula Serif (1988)
Lunatix (1989)
Oblong (1989, with Rudy Vanderlans)
Senator (1989)
Variex (1989, with Rudy Vanderlans)
Citizen (1990)
Elektrix (1990)
Totally Gothic (1990)
Totally Glyphic (1990)
Triplex (1990, italic by John Downer)
Journal (1991)

Zuzanna Licko is a Czechoslovakian who emigrated to the United States in 1968 and graduated in graphic communication from the University of California in Berkeley. With Rudy Vanderlans she forms the design team Emigré Design, and together they produce the influential journal Emigré, in which Licko, as the type designer, has advanced fundamental ideas on the role of computer technology in type design. All her typefaces are designed on, and for, the Macintosh and in 1985 they set up Emigre Fonts to market their typefaces and those by other young designers.

Her concern with low resolution systems and their neglect by type designers has led to the production of typefaces designed specifically for this purpose; these include Oakland, Emigré, Emperor and Universal.

She has also designed Zenith, Berkeley and Matrix which are intended for high resolution systems, and all her typefaces are now available in PostScript format.

RCE

LINOTYPE & Linotye Paul   USA & GB

The first hot-metal, line-casting machine was installed at the *New York Tribune* in 1886 by its inventor and pioneer Ottmar Mergenthaler, and in the same year the name 'Line-o-type' was coined, a name which was to be associated with every major development in mechanical composition for the next 100 years.

At the close of the nineteenth century the advancement of literacy on both sides of the Atlantic had swelled the demand for newspapers, periodicals and books, and in turn had created an equal demand for fast and inexpensive typesetting. Mergenthaler's invention met the challenge of this new market in every detail, and in order to develop and exploit the new technology the firm of Linotype was founded in the United States in 1890 and its counterpart in the United Kingdom in 1895.

The year 1895 was also the year in which Theodore L.De Vinne first used the typeface Century for his popular *Century* Magazine. Century had been cut for De Vinne by Linn Boyd Benton, the inventor of the automatic punch-cutting machine. Benton's invention had played a decisive part in the advancement of the Linotype principle, because, for the first time, it had made possible the rapid production of metal matrices, a crucial factor that Mergenthaler had been quick o recognise.

The Linotype machine, together with its competitors, the MONOTYPE single-type casting and composing machine and the Typograph, was to dominate the market until the arrival of photocomposition in the 1960s. Meanwhile, in 1900, D. Stempel AG and Mergenthaler GmbH had contracted to produce matrices for the Linotype machine and the early years of the century saw the company issue many new and revised typefaces under the guidance of George W.JONES who was appointed printing advisor to the company in 1921. Among these were Granjon (1924), Georgian (1925), Estienne (1926) and Venezia (1928).

In 1925 Linotype introduced Ionic for newspaper composition and within eighteen months it was adopted by no less than 3,000 publications. Ionic was cut under the direction of C.H.GRIFFITH, as were all Linotype faces from 1915 to 1949, and such was its popularity that it soon stimulated a whole new series of newspaper types which became known as the 'Legibility Group'. Designers working for Mergenthaler linotype in this period included W.A.DWIGGINS, (Metro 1929-30, Caledonia 1938), and Rudolf RUZICKA, (Fairfield 1939).

In 1932 Linotype issued Times New Roman, the type commissioned by *The Times* in London and produced under the supervision of Stanley MORISON.

Walter TRACY, the eminent type designer and writer, joined Linotype in 1947 and designed Jubilee (1953), Adsans (1959) and, for *The Daily Telegraph,* Linotype Modern (1969). Other designers working for the various international divisions of Linotype at this time were C.H.Griffith, Hermann ZAPF, Reynolds STONE and Sem L.HARTZ.

The first Linofilm photocomposing machine was previewed at The International Printing Exhibition in London in 1955 and the first production model was installed at *National Geographic Magazine* in 1959. In the UK, Linofilm photocomposition equipment extended to book production by 1962 with the publication of a biography of Scott Fitzgerald, set by William Clowes & Sons and published by Bodley Head.

In the following decades the pace of change accelerated markedly when Linotype and CBS in America cooperated on cathode ray tube (CRT) technology. First came the Linotron 1010 typesetter which was introduced in 1965 and installed at the US Government Printing Office in 1967. Then, in the same year, came the Computer-only Linofilm typesetter, an important step on the road to full computer compatibility which

Square base Linotype of 1889. (Photo: St. Bride Printing Library)

was successfully achieved a few years later with the Linotron 505, a development of the Purdy MacIntosh Filmsetter 1001. In 1969 Linotype Paul was formed in the UK when K.S.Paul purchased Linotype & Machinery Ltd. a company which had been formed in 1903. The software package CORA was introduced at this time, followed in the late 1970s by a progression of new products notably the Linotron 202 and the much imi-tated ATP software.

In 1984 the Linotronic 300 laser photosetter was intro-duced, with Linotype Laser Fonts encoded in outline form, a machine which has become pre-eminent in its field.

The company now manufactures a range of POSTSCRIPT compatible imagesetters and the Mergenthaler Type Library is licensed to ADOBE Systems Inc. for production in PostScript format.

RCE

Herb LUBALIN   1918-81   USA

Avant Garde Gothic (1970, with Tom Carnese)
Lubalin Graph (1974)
Serif Gothic (1974)

Herb Lubalin was one of the most charismatic figures in design and typography in America in the years following World War II. Admired as a prodigious worker with a vast out-put, most of his design solutions relied upon typography for their effect and to achieve this end he would often rewrite clients copy, generally to good effect it is said! In the early days his typefaces, and indeed those of ITC in general, were aimed at display advertising rather than text setting and they became internationally known through the influential and stylish magazine *U&lc*, the house journal of ITC which Lubalin not only designed but also edited.

Born in New York City of humble Russo-German parent-age—his father was a classical trumpet player, his mother a singer—Lubalin was fortunate in obtaining a non-fee paying position at the Cooper Union School of Art and Architecture were he graduated in 1939.

After a spell as Art Director at Deutsch & Shea Advertising and Reis Advertising he became Art Director and eventually Vice President & Creative Director of Sudler & Hennessey, a studio specialising in pharmaceutical advertising and pro-motions.

By 1964 he had entered a partnership with Aaron Burns as Executive Vice-President of Lubalin & Burns, a name which became synonymous with the most avant-garde work in design and typography of the period. It was this partnership, in cooperation with Edward Rondthaler, that gave birth to the concept of the ITC: an organisation without any manu-facturing facilities which nevertheless became the world's largest institutional supplier of typefaces. In the early days many of the typefaces were designed by Lubalin himself or by close associates such as Ed BENGUIAT.

In addition to ITC and typeface design, Lubalin became internationally known for his work as art director on the magazines *Eros* and *Avant Garde* which became famous as much for their design as for their content. The typeface Avante Garde, with its extended set of ligatures, began life as a masthead for the magazine.

RCB

Charles MALIN   1883-1955   F

Charles Malin, the celebrated French punch-cutter, worked for the leading type designers of his day including Eric Gill, Giovanni Mardersteig and Frederic Warde.

When Stanley Morison commissioned Gill's Perpetua, he turned to Malin to interpret the drawings rather than use the pantograph. Only when satisfied with the result, was the type handed over to the MONOTYPE works for production. Morison had first met Malin as a result of his interest in Frederic Warde's Arrighi Italic.

The designer with whom Malin had the longest collaboration was Giovanni Mardersteig the German printer and scholar who spent the greater part of his life working in Verona. It was a fruitful partnership and the two worked together for 24 years. Malin cut most of Mardersteig's types and although Mardersteig outlived him by twenty years he never produced another type design.

RCE

Aldus MANUTIUS   1450-1515   I
& Francesco GRIFFO   died c.1518   I

The types of the prolific Renaissance printer and publisher Aldus Manutius and his punch-cutter Francesco Griffo improved upon the earlier JENSON type and, because they were so attractive and legible, became the model for the next 250 years. The invention of italic type is generally ascribed to Manutius and Griffo and made its first appearance in a 1501 edition of Virgil.

Manutius was born in 1450 in the Duchy of Sermoneta. He spent the early part of his career working under the patronage of the Count Alberto Pio, Prince of Carpi, but left Carpi for Venice in 1489 to further his ambition of publishing Greek

·lassics in the original. While the market for Latin editions in
taly was overcrowded, the opposite was true of Greek works
ınd in Venice he would have access to collections of fine man-
ıscripts. His first publications came out in 1484: an edition of
he *Galeomyomachia & Musæus' De Herone & Leandro.*

His chief interest was promoting the study of Greek which
ıe did through his publications and through founding an
Academy dedicated to this end, in 1500. His Greek types—
ıased on the handwriting of his friend Marcus Musurius—
ıave been widely criticised, their chief fault is in the number
ıf contractions and ligatures they use.

In his early Greek books, any roman type needed was
ıought from other printers and Manutius' first original
ıoman type did not appear until 1495 in Cardinal Bembo's *De
Aetna*, which Stanley MORISON demonstrated, was the basis
ıor Claude GARAMOND's types. The type was revised before its
ıse in the *Hypnerotomachia Poliphili* of 1499, when a new, larg-
ır and lighter upper case was added.

The first Aldine italic appeared in a book in1501. and was
ıased on a script used in the Papal Chancery. Griffo was to
ıesign two others: one for the printer Geronimo Soncino for
ıis *Petrach* of 1503, and one for himself. Griffo used this when
ıe began to publish small editions on his own account when
ıe returned to his native Bologna after Manutius' death.
Although successful as an idea, italics by later designers followed other models.

Aldus published on a large scale (a letter of his refers to
1000 or more volumes a month) and amassed a considerable
fortune, aided by a number of copyrights and monopolies
which the College of Venice had granted him. His imprint was
a dolphin and anchor. He helped to popularise many works by
using an octavo format which made his books cheaper and
more portable but he fell out with many of the scholars who
lent him old manuscripts because of his habit of using such
manuscripts in the press room and marking them up with
instructions rather than having copies made for this purpose.
Francesco Griffo also had a dispute with Aldus, whom he
claimed had not given him sufficient credit for the types, this
dispute over authorship of the so called Aldine types was later
taken up by type scholars.

Aldus died aged 65 in his house in the Venetian printing
quarter of San Paternian and his body lay in state there sur-
rounded by copies of his books. Francesco Griffo died some
time around 1518/19. The cause and exact date of his death

Aldus Manutius, page from *Hypnerotomachia Poliphili* by Francesco Colonna, 1499. (photo: St. Bride Printing Library)

Per laquale cofa, principiai pofcia ragioneuolmente fufpicare & credere peruenuto nella uaftiffima Hercynia filua. Et quiui altro non effere che latibuli de nocente fere,& cauernicole de noxii animali & de feuiente belue. Et percio cum maximo terriculo dubitaua, di effere fencia alcuna defenfa, & fencia auederme dilaniato da fetofo & dentato Apro, Quale Charidemo,ouero da furente, & famato Vro, Ouero da fibillante ferpe & da fremendi lupi incurfanti miferamente dimembrabondo lurcare ue deffe le carne mie. Dicio dubitádo ifpagurito, Iui propofi (damnata qua lunque pigredine) piu non dimorare,& de trouare exito & euadere gli oc correnti pericoli, & de folicitare gli gia fofpefi & difordinati paffi, fpeffe fi ate negli radiconi da terra fcoperti cefpitádo, de qui, & de li peruagabon do errante, hora ad lato dextro,& mo al finiftro, tal hora retrogrado, & tal fiata antigrado, infcio & oue non fapendo meare, peruenuto in Salto & dumeto & fenticofo loco tutto granfiato dalle frafche,& da fpinofi pru nuli,& da lintractabile fructo la facia offenfa. Et per gli mucronati carde ti,& altri fpini lacerata la toga & ritinuta impediua pigritando la tentata fuga. Oltra quefto non uedendo delle amaeftreuole pedate indicio alcu no,ne tritulo di femita,non mediocremente diffufo & dubiofo, piu folicitamente acceleraua, Si che per gli celeri paffi, fi per el meridionale æfto quale per el moto corporale facto calido, tutto de fudore humefacto el
fredo

re not known, but it seems likely that he was hanged for
killing his brother-in-law, which he did with an iron bar in
May 1518 during a fight.

Monotype have produced two faces based on Manutius'
designs. Poliphilus is a facsimile of the type used in the *Hypnerotomachia Poliphili* and, rather than use the unsatisfactory
Aldine italic, one based on the 1539 italic of ARRIGHI was chosen and named after the printer who originally used it: Blado.
Bembo (based on the *De Aetna* types), is a revival, regularised
for the twentieth century and one of a programme instigated
by Stanley Morison. It has proved very popular as a book typeface and other manufacturers now supply versions. Bembo
narrow italic was designed by Alfred FAIRBANK.

SR

Hans (or Giovanni) MARDERSTEIG   1892-1977   D

Fontana (1936, see A.WILSON)
Dante (1954)

Hans Mardersteig was both a scholar and a printer, he re-
searched into Renaissance printing, focusing particularly on
the work of Francesco GRIFFO. He is best known for the work
of the private press which he founded, the 'Officina Bodoni',
but after World War II he extended his operations to include
a commercial press, the Stamparia Valdonega. Mardersteig
received the Gutenberg prize in 1968.

Mardersteig was born in Weimar in 1892. As a young man
he edited an art magazine *Genius* but because he suffered
from tuberculosis he was advised to leave Germany for the
better climate of Switzerland. Once there, in 1923 he established his own private press in Montagnola which he was to
call the Officina Bodoni' after Giovanni Battista Bodoni the
famous Parma printer.

The Officina produced works on type and printing, poetry
and literary classics, using handset types on a hand-press.
Among Mardersteig's types were castings he had made from
original Bodoni matrices.

Work printed by the press includes *The Calligraphic Models
of Ludovico Degli Arrighi* which Mardersteig printed for Frederic WARDE using Warde's new Arrighi type, and Stanley MORI-
SON wrote the introduction. Mardersteig and Morison shared
an interest in the history of types and calligraphy and were to
maintain a long and friendly correspondence.

In 1927 the Officina moved to Verona and, to coincide with

the move, Mardersteig italianized his name. From this time onwards he was known as Giovanni.

Many of the types used at the Officina were of Mardersteig's design. They were cut for him by the Paris punch-cutter Charles Malin (a productive collaboration) and although Mardersteig continued working until he was 86 his type designing ceased with Malin's death in 1955. Mardersteig's best known types are Dante and Fontana. Designed not for the Officina, but for the exclusive use of the publishers William Collins of Glasgow, Fontana is a revival of a 1760 type cut by Alexander WILSON of Glasgow, which itself is based on BASKERVILLE's types. Cut by Monotype in 1957 it was not released to the trade until 1961. Dante was designed for the Officina Bodoni in 1954 and later cut for Monotype. A popular type it was quickly taken up by other printers.

SR

William MARTIN, see BULMER

John Henry MASON   1875-1951   GB

Imprint (1913)

J.H.Mason was the editor of the highly influential British journal *The Imprint* and was head of the Book Production department at the Central School of Arts & Crafts in London where he taught from 1905.

The son of an admiral's daughter and a carriage builder for the London General Omnibus Company, he served his apprenticeship as a compositor with the London book printers Ballantyne. Despite having started work at thirteen Mason was a notable scholar, mostly self- taught. At 25 he joined the Doves Press, owned by Emery WALKER and Cobden-Sanderson, and worked as a compositor for the Doves Press *Folio Bible* of 1905. He also worked as an adviser to the Cranach Press at Weimar.

The journal *The Imprint* was founded by friends: Gerard Meynell, a director of the Westminster Press which printed and published the journal; Edward JOHNSTON who was the lettering editor and F. Ernest Jackson, an expert on lithography and illustrative techniques. An advisory board included professor W.R.Lethaby who founded The Central School, and Theodore Low DE VINNE. The aims of *The Imprint* were unashamedly high, in the first issue they wrote:

> We care for our trade and wish to raise it to its worthy place among the crafts...we shall aim at improving and spreading technical knowledge...our standards will be high, and our use of them severe: our judgments will be critical and exacting.

The typeface used, Imprint Old Face, was specially cut by Monotype to Mason's brief and was based on Caslon Old Face. Imprint, however, was designed for mechanical composition and printing on dry papers, it is altogether more regular and precise. It was the first type to be designed specifically for machine composition and was to prove that the new technologies—pantographic punch-cutting and machine composition—could produce results that rivalled in appearance the best hand-composed examples of the past.

However, *The Imprint* was not a financial success and after just nine issues it ceased publication in November 1913, albeit with reputation intact. Mason continued teaching despite deteriorating eyesight and retired in 1941. In 1936 he became one of the first Royal Designers for Industry.

SR

José MENDOZA y Almeida   20thC   F

Pascal (1960)
Photina (1971) **182**

A French designer of Spanish descent, José Mendoza was apprenticed as a photoengraver at Cliché Union in Paris, one of the first companies to adopt Monophoto filmsetting. From 1954 to 1959 he was assistant to Roger EXCOFFON at the Fonderie Olive'Paris office and afterwards became a freelance designer. His best known typeface is Photina, released by the MONOTYPE Corporation in 1971. It was only their third typeface designed exclusively for filmsetting and was designed to work harmoniously with Adrian FRUTIGER's Univers series.

RCE

Oldrîch MENHART   1897-1962   CS

Menhart Antiqua & Kursive (1932)
Menhart (1938) **143**
Menhart Roman (1939)
Triga (1951)
Ceska Uncial

Figural
Manuscript
Monument
Parliament
Standard
Victory

The Czech language, because it is the most heavily accented modern language, can appear very fragmented on the page. This problem was to be a major preoccupation of Oldrîch Menhart throughout his life, and although it had been addressed by others in the past, notably Preissing, no satisfactory solution had been found. Menhart deals with the problem to some extent in his first book, *The first Czech school of ornamental letterforms,* which he produced with Karl Mirazek at the age of 24.

Oldrîch Menhart was born in Prague the son of a master goldsmith who came from a long line of craftsmen. Oldrîch was the youngest of four sons and, like his brothers, he was taught drawing, carving and engraving by his father. In 1911 he was apprenticed as a compositor with a printer in Prague and in his spare time he studied letters in church sepulchres and church yards. In 1915 he entered a period of five years' military service.

In 1924 the Czech Institute awarded him a stipend which enabled him to travel to Antwerp and then to Paris, where he saw the Imprimerie National. During this trip he made contact with the BAUER foundry. By 1929 he had become very dissatisfied with the state printing office in Prague where he was working and left to become a freelance calligrapher and book designer. In 1930 he produced his first type designs, Codex Antiqua and Kursive, which were strongly influenced by Walter TIEMANN and Peter BEHRENS and which were later produced by the Bauer foundry in 1932 as Menhart Antiqua and Kursive.

Many of his types show a strong calligraphic influence, particularly in the italics, and Manuscript is based closely on his own handwriting.

Menhart continued to work until declining health and poor eyesight prevented him from doing so. His last letterforms, the swash caps for Figural Italic were issued in 1962, the year of his death.

RCE

Robert Hunter MIDDLETON 1898-1985 USA

Eusebius italic & versions (1923-29)
Ludlow Black (1924)
Cameo (1927)
Record Gothic (1927-60) **288**
Delphian Open Titling (1928)
Stellar (1929)
Tempo (1930-42) **264,**
Karnak (1931-42)
Lafayette (1932) **595**
Mayfair Cursive (1932)
Eden (1934)
Mandate (1934)
Umbra (1935) **661**
Stencil (1938) **575**
Radiant (1940) **609**
Samson (1940)
Flair (1941)
Admiral Script (1953)
Florentine Cursive (1956) **605**
Formal Script (1956)
Condensed Gothic Outline (1953)
Wave (1962)
Square Gothic

& Ernst F.DETTERER 1888-1947 D

Eusebius roman (1923)

The German designer, teacher and calligrapher, Ernst F.Detterer came to America where he became associated with the revival of interest in the typefaces of the fifteenth-century Venetian printer Nicolas JENSON. Working for the Ludlow Typographic Company in Chicago, he designed a typeface based on these much admired Jenson models. This typeface was created in 1923 and was called Eusebius, a name chosen because Eusebius Pamphili was the author of the first book in which Jenson's type appeared for the first time in 1470.

While lecturing on the printing arts at the Chicago Art Institute Detterer met Robert Hunter Middleton, who was a student in his class. Detterer and Middleton started to work together on the new typeface and subsequently Middleton was employed by Ludlow to see the typeface through its production stages. Middleton stayed with the foundry and by

1929 he had the created matching bold, italic and open versions of Eusebius. From then until his retirement in 1971 he produced nearly 100 typefaces including many of their best known sans serif and display types.

Middleton was also infiuential in the revival of interest in the work of Thomas Bewick (1753-1828), the celebrated English wood-engraver, whose work he printed in his spare time.

RCE

Max MIEDINGER   d.1980   CH

Pro Arte (1954)
Neue Haas Grotesk/Helvetica (1957-) **279, 422, 477, 493-4, 529-530, 620, 624**
Horizontal (1964)

Max Miedinger of Zürich was an in-house designer with the HAAS Foundry in Munchenstein, Switzerland. His most famous typeface is Helvetica, currently the most widely used sans serif, which was designed in 1956.

Edouard Hoffman of Haas had asked Miedinger to adapt the existing Haas Grotesk to bring it into line with current taste. Haas Grotesk had its origins in the nineteenth-century German Grotesques like Berthold's Akzindenz Grotesk. The type, which was created from Miedinger's china-ink drawings seemed like a new design in its own right, rather than an old one with minor retouching as had been the original plan. Although designed with the home market in mind Neue Haas Grotesk, as it was then called, proved popular further afield. When Stempel AG. in Germany, released the face in 1961 they called it Helvetica, the traditional Latin name for Switzerland in order to capitalise on the fashion for Swiss typography. Although not planned as a family of many weights like Adrian FRUTIGER's Univers, the Helvetica family has been added to over the past 30 years and it is available on most typesetting systems.

The two other faces of Miedinger's are Pro Arte, a revival of a nineteenth-century poster typeface, and Horizontal, a heavy square titling face.

SR

John MILES, see BANKS

MILLER & RICHARD Foundry   GB

This famous Scottish foundry was started in 1809 by George Miller who had worked at WILSON's Glasgow foundry before setting up in business on his own in Edinburgh. When his son-in-law Walter Richard became a partner in 1832 the firm became known as Miller & Richard. The company developed rapidly and supplied type to many newspapers including *The Times* in London.

In its early days some of the modern fonts supplied by Miller & Richard were cut by Richard AUSTIN before he set up his own company in London. In 1852 Alexander PHEMISTER, who had trained as a punch-cutter with William Grandison, joined the company as a punch-cutter and type designer, as a result of which several new series of romans were issued. These type faces proved extremely popular and were in great demand by English publishers.

At the Great Exhibition of 1851 Miller & Richard showed a setting of Gray's *Elegy* in the smallest type ever made in Britain at that time, about $3^1/_2$ point. The 32 verses were set in two columns, each 23 ems deep. The company was the first in Britain to introduce machinery for the casting of type.

When the company closed in 1952 many of the moulds and type fonts were taken over by the STEPHENSON BLAKE foundry.

RCE

No. 322—**3/6**

No. 389—**3/-**

Movable and electro cheques from Miller & Richard's *Printing type specimens*, c.1925.   (Photo: St. Bride Printing Library)

MONOTYPE CORPORATION plc
& Lanston Monotype Corporation   GB & USA

At the end of the nineteenth century the spread of literacy on both sides of the Atlantic had created a vast new market for printed material, particularly newspapers and periodicals. It was a market that the old typecasting and handsetting methods of the day, which had not significantly changed for many years, were barely adequate to satisfy. Consequently, one of the greatest technical challenges at that time was the invention of a method of rapid, automatic type composition.

The potential rewards for a successful solution to this problem were very great indeed, and it has been estimated that some 200 inventors worked for 100 years in an attempt to find a solution. Into this picture came a remarkable man, Talbert Lanston. He had served as a Sergeant in the American Civil War and then, for 22 years, as a government pension clerk, during which time he had graduated from the Columbia Law School to be admitted to practice at the bar of the Supreme Court. Lanston was also a gifted inventor. His early inventions included an adjustable horseshoe, a mail-bag lock and an adding machine. He first conceived the idea for a type-composing machine after inspecting a Hollerith Tabulator, and rapidly formulated three principles for a successful solution. These principles were: the keyboard must be separate, encoding information onto a punched tape; each piece of type must be individually produced (not as a line, as in the LINOTYPE machine); each line of type must be mathematically justified.

Inspired by the commercial success of Ottmar Mergenthaler's Linotype machine in 1886, backers were soon found for Lanston's project and in 1887 patents were taken out and The Lanston Monotype Company was formed. In 1893 an early model was exhibited at the Columbian World Fair in Chicago and production of the first 50 machines commenced in the following year. Meanwhile, an important change was made to the design by the company's production manager, John Sellers Bancroft, who replaced the original cold die-stamping component with a hot metal caster, the same principle that had been used on Mergenthaler's Linotype machine.

By 1887 the only obstacle to progress was a serious lack of investment which threatened to halt development. In a quest for funds, J.Maury Dove, the company's first president, and H.M.Duncan, the technical director, set off across the Atlantic hoping to raise capital in England. As luck would have it, their problem was solved before the ship had docked: one of the passengers on board was the Earl of Dunraven who was sufficiently astute to form a syndicate to purchase the British rights for £200,000 (one million dollars), at that time a record sum for such and investment. As a result, The Lanston Monotype Corporation was founded in England in 1897 and a factory was built at Salfords in Surrey where production commenced in 1902. The name changed to the Monotype Corporation Ltd. in 1931.

The inherent technical advantages of the Monotype machine, particularly its ability to kern, gave it significant advantages over the Linotype machine, but a major problem was the lack of fine typefaces. The cutting of Imprint in 1912, the first original type design to be cut for mechanical composition, and of Plantin in 1913 had demonstrated that the Monotype machine could compete on quality with traditional typefoundries. Consequently, in 1922, Stanley MORISON was appointed as typographical advisor as part of an ambitious type-cutting programme which in the following years was to provide a unique and important collection of book and periodical faces for mechanical composition. During the 1920s and 30s Baskerville, Bell, Bembo, Centaur, Ehrhart, Fournier, Garamond, Gill Sans, Perpetua, Poliphilus and Times New Roman were cut.

Meanwhile, in America the fortunes of Monotype had not been as good as those of its British counterpart and after several changes of ownership Monotype eventually became part of AMERICAN TYPEFOUNDERS' until, in 1983, what was left was sold to Mackenzie-Harris, a San Francisco typefounder.

In the UK however, Monotype became increasingly involved with filmsetting starting with the Monophoto filmsetters in 1955, and later with the Monotype filmlettering machine in 1963.

In the middle 1960s a growing interest in computer-aided type setting led the company to set up a marketing arrangement with the Swiss GSA modular system which led to the introduction of a computer input perforator and to the development of tape conversion equipment.

In 1976 the company introduced the world's first laser typesetting system, the Lasercomp, which was capable of full-page imagesetting. This has been succeeded by a range of products which includes dedicated typesetters, PostScript compatible imagesetters and graphics manipulation systems.

The type library now has over 2,000 faces (including 200 non-latins) of which more than 400 are now available in PostScript format.

RCE

Isaac MOORE,
see FRY

Stanley MORISON   1889-1967   GB

Times New Roman (1932) **52/53**

Stanley Morison designed only one typeface, Times New Roman, but through his work at Monotype, as a founder of *The Fleuron,* and as a frequent writer on type, he was one of the most influential figures in British typography.

Morison was born near Wanstead in London and grew up in an atmosphere of poverty but with intellectual stimulation from his mother. Leaving school at 14, he studied on Saturdays at the British Museum and applied for his first type-related job after reading the printing supplement in *The Times,* 10 September 1908. He became editorial assistant on the *Imprint,* a journal founded and edited by J.H.MASON and others. Like *The Fleuron* which he founded with Oliver Simon in 1919, the Imprint was not a great financial success, but both publications did a great deal to raise awareness of, and an interest in, typography.

After the *Imprint* Morison worked for the Pelican Press and Cloister Press before joining Monotype early in 1923. Two years later he took on the extra post of typographical consultant to the Cambridge University Press.

Monotype had begun to revive historic types before Morison joined them but he brought an informed enthusiasm to the work, and although there was no systematic programme as such, the revivals cut during his time at the Corporation eventually covered all periods of typographic history. Among them were Baskerville, Bell, Bembo, Ehrhardt and Fournier. His interest in types also embraced contemporary designs and he was responsible for commissioning original faces from Eric GILL and Jan VAN KRIMPEN.

In 1929, Morison's involvement with The Times began when he criticised the paper's typography to the management, who responded by asking him to improve it. His research into John BELL had already given him a knowledge of newspaper typography and after experimenting with Perpetua and Plantin he designed a new face based on a GRANJON model. A draughtsman from *The Times,* Victor Lardent, did the finished drawings for the face which first appeared in the newspaper on 3 October 1932. A year later it was made available to the trade and quickly established itself as a standard book typeface. It was used until changing technology—phototypesetting and web-offset reproduction—made it unsuitable, when it was replaced by Walter TRACY's Times Europa.

Morison also wrote widely on type. His many books include *Four centuries of fine printing, First principles in typography* and *A tally of types.* He was made a Fellow of the British Academy in 1954 and a Royal Designer for Industry in 1960.

SR

William MORRIS   1834-96   GB

Golden (1890)
Troy (1892)
Chaucer (1893)

William Morris, notable as a socialist and writer, was a key figure in the Arts & Crafts movement of the late nineteenth century. He did not involve himself in printing and typography until he was approaching the end of his career. He first began training as an architect, later switched to painting then worked in divers branches of design, being perhaps best known for his wallpapers and printed textiles. The inspiration for this new interest in typography was a lantern lecture on letter forms given to the Arts & Crafts Exhibition Society on 15 November 1888 by Emery WALKER.

In December 1889 Morris asked Walker to go into partnership with him as a printer; although Walker declined a partnership he agreed to act as an adviser. A year later Morris founded the Kelmscott Press; it was always intended as a small private press; he used his own types, hand presses, and printed on dampened handmade paper.

Morris designed two types for the Press, both cut by Edward PRINCE who had already cut types for Emery Walker. Golden was the result of his early drawings of venetian types and was the most influential of his designs. It was based on Jenson's *Pliny* of 1476 and a history of Florence printed by Jacobus Rubeus in the same year. Although his models are light venetians Morris's own tastes led him to give the letter forms a darker, more mediæval feel. He planned to use it for an edition of the *Golden Legend,* hence the name. Golden sparked off the interest in Jenson revivals, and his resistance to offering Golden for commercial use led to foundries cutting their own Jenson inspired faces. A pre-1900 version was ATF's Nicolas Jenson.

His other face (an informal blackletter) was cut for use in the *Kelmscott Chaucer.* This face came in two sizes known as Troy and Chaucer.The *Kelmscott Chaucer* is the Press's best known work. Sir Edward Burne-Jones, Pre-Raphaelite painter supplied the illustrations. It took four years to produce, the last years of Morris's life. The Chaucer was completed on 6 May 1896 and Morris died after a long illness in October of that year.

Sydney Cockerell and F.S.Ellis took over and ran the press for a further two years. The Kelmscott Press, in the eight years of its operation issued 52 books in 66 volumes.

SR

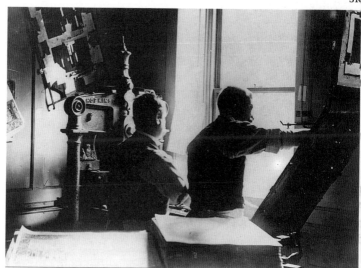

Printing the Kelmscott Press *Chaucer,* c.1895.
(Photo: The Walker Collection at St. Bride Printing Library)

Robin **NICHOLAS** b.1947 GB

Nimrod (1980) **122**

Robin Nicholas, who was born in Westerham, Kent, joined Monotype in 1965 after training as an engineering draughtsman. He has been the manager of their type drawing office since 1982.

Between 1978 and 1980 he designed Nimrod, a group of related roman faces designed for newspaper text, headlines and small ads. Nimrod was first used in the *Leicester Mercury* and later taken up by several other papers including *The Guardian* (for leaders), *The Daily Telegraph* and *Today*. Nimrod was one of the first typefaces to be designed for Monotype's Lasercomp system and was widely praised for its readability. RON CARPENTER assisted with the design of the italic.

Robin Nicholas has supervised the design or revival of many Monotype faces including Arial, Clarion, Bell, Centaur, Janson, Van Dijck and Walbaum.

SR

Aldo NOVARESE   b.1920   I

Athenæum* (1945) **134**
Augustea (1951, with A.BUTTI) **171, 409, 416**
Microgramma (1952, with A.Butti)
Fontanesi (1954)
Egizio (1955-8)
Juliet (1955)
Garaldus (1956)
Slogan (1957)
Recta (1958-61)
Estro (1961)
Eurostile (1962) **291**
Novarese (1980) **226, 464**
Cigogna (with A.Butti)

The designer of the much-maligned Eurostile/Microgramma, Aldo Novarese is also known as a writer on type. He has written two books on typography and contributed to a number of design and graphics publications.

Born in Italy he studied at the Turin Graphic School and has designed most of his types for the Art Studio of the Nebiolo foundry, also in Turin. He joined the foundry when he was sixteen and became Art Director in 1952. Many of the earlier types he worked on were designed in a productive partnership with Alessandro Butti. These include Augustea and Microgramma which, with the addition of a lower case, became Eurostile in 1962. The Garamond-based Garaldus, takes its name from a category in the Vox system of type classification. In 1980 he designed the type that bears his name, Novarese, for the HAAS foundry.

SR

Mike PARKER   b.1929   GB

Although born in England, Mike Parker has worked for many years in America and until 1981 was Director of Typography for Mergenthaler LINOTYPE where he was responsible for adding some 1,000 typefaces to the Mergenthaler Type Library. As well as many type revivals and Russian, Arabic Hebrew and Greek faces, he also commissioned original faces from leading designers including Matthew CARTER, Adrian FRUTIGER and Herman ZAPF.

He left Linotype in 1981 and with Matthew Carter he set up BITSTREAM Inc., the Cambridge (Mass.)-based digital type foundry specialising in the development of fonts for desktop publishing applications.

He is also a director of The Company, a typographical consultancy.

RCH

The PEIGNOT family   F
Gustave   1839-99
Georges   1872-1914
Charles   1897-1983
& DEBERNY & PEIGNOT Foundry

[Peignot (1937, see A.M.CASSANDRE)]

The great French foundry of Deberny & Peignot is the result of the amalgamation of two separate strands which did not come together until 1923. The earliest of these strands was the Deberny foundry which owes its existence to Honoré de Balzac who, in 1827, had the idea of forming his own publishing and printing company, primarily to produce his own books. Not wishing to do anything by halves, Balzac, then only 28, decided to include a type foundry in the enterprise which he did by forming an association with Laurent, an experienced foundry foreman. Alas, in a very short time the whole project failed, but luckily Laurent managed to salvage what remained of the type foundry, leaving the rest to Balzac and the pursuing creditors.

That the foundry survived at all is due to the assistance Laurent received from Alexandre de Berny, then only nineteen, who took an active role in the business and eventually bought out Laurent's share in 1840. De Berny built up the business with great success over a period of fifty years until it became one of the foremost foundries of its time. In 1877 he

eignot by A.M.Cassandre, used in *Missal*, Paris 1937.
hoto: St. Bride Printing Library)

---

566   **Die 24 Aug. · S. Bartholomæi Apostoli**

Postcommunio

Quæsumus, omnipotens Deus : ut, qui cælestia alimenta percepimus, intercedente beato Philippo Confessore tuo, per hæc contra omnia adversa muniamur. Per Dominum.

Pro Vigilia S. Bartholomæi Postcommunio

Sancti Apostoli tui Bartholomæi quæsumus, Domine, supplicatione placatus : et veniam nobis tribue, et remedia sempiterna concede. Per Dominum.

Et in fine Missæ, legitur Evangelium de Vigilia juxta Rubricas :

Sequentia sancti Evangelii secundum Joannem

Joann. 15, 12-16

In illo tempore : Dixit Jesus discipulis suis : Hoc est præceptum meum, ut diligatis invicem, sicut dilexi vos. Majorem hac dilectionem nemo habet, ut animam suam ponat quis pro amicis suis. Vos amici mei estis, si feceritis quæ ego præcipio vobis. Jam non dicam vos servos : quia servus nescit quid faciat dominus ejus. Vos autem dixi amicos : quia omnia quæcumque audivi a Patre meo, nota feci vobis. Non vos me elegistis : sed ego elegi vos, et posui vos, ut eatis, et fructum afferatis : et fructus vester maneat : ut quodcumque petieritis Patrem in nomine meo, det vobis.

Ubi adest obligatio Chori, lecta post Tertiam extra Chorum Missa de Festo sine Commemoratione Vigiliæ, in Choro post Nonam dicitur Missa de Vigilia, ut infra ; et de Vigilia dici possunt etiam Missæ Privatæ cum 2ª tantum Oratione Festi.

EADEM DIE 23 AUGUSTI

IN VIGILIA SANCTI BARTHOLOMÆI

APOSTOLI

Missa Ego autem, de Communi in Vigiliis Apostolorum 1*, cum 2ª Oratione de sancta Maria Concede 36*, et 3ª contra persecutores Ecclesiæ, vel pro Papa 38*

DIE 24 AUGUSTI

SANCTI BARTHOLOMÆI

APOSTOLI

Introitus   Ps. 138, 17

Mihi autem nimis honorati sunt amici tui, Deus : nimis confortatus est principatus eorum. Ps. ibid., 1-2. Domine, probasti me, et cognovisti me : tu cognovisti sessionem meam, et resurrectionem meam. ℣. Gloria Patri. Mihi.

Oratio

Omnipotens sempiterne Deus, qui hujus diei venerandam sanctamque lætitiam in beati Apostoli tui Bartholomæi festivitate tribuisti : da Ecclesiæ tuæ, quæsumus ; et amare quod credidit et prædicare quod docuit. Per Dominum.

Lectio Epistolæ beati Pauli Apostoli ad Corinthios I Cor. 12, 27-31

Fratres : Vos estis corpus Christi et membra de membro. Et quosdam quidem posuit Deus in Ecclesia primum apostolos, secundo prophetas, tertio doctores, deinde virtutes, exinde gratias curationum, opitulationes, gubernationes, genera linguarum, interpretationes sermonum. Numquid omnes apostoli ? numquid

---

was joined by a new partner, Charles Tuleu, who later succeeded him and who was probably responsible for the best of the work produced at the foundry at this time. In 1914 a M. Girard became president of the company which became known as Girard & Co.

The other strand in this chronicle starts in 1865 when Gustave Peignot bought out a small foundry established by

Leclerc in 1842. In 1881 the foundry was further expanded by the acquisition of three small foundries, Petibon, Cochard and David, so that when Gustave died he was able to leave his son Georges a fine collection of classic faces and an equally fine reputation.

Georges Peignot started the policy of commissioning new typefaces from leading artists and designers and during his leadership outstanding designers such as Eugene Grasset and Georges AURIOL created successful new faces for the company.

In 1913 he successfully re-introduced the eighteenth-century typefaces of the great French engraver Nicolas COCHIN. With his son Charles he supervised the cutting of the Deberny and Peignot Garamond (1912-28) from the Caractères de l'Université of the Imprimerie Royale (believed to be by Garamond but later credited to JANNON). Georges Peignot died during World War I. His son Charles, a grandson of the founder, entered the family business in 1919, and four years later the company merged with Girard & Co (the name of the De Berny Foundry from 1914) and became known as Deberny & Peignot.

Within a few years of entering the business Charles Peignot began to demonstrate the skill which was to make the Deberny & Peignot foundry famed throughout the world. This was achieved by broadening the range of faces and commissioning leading contemporary artists and designers to create new ones. Faces such as Cassandre's Acier Noir, Bifur, and Peignot were produced in the 1920s and 1930s and were rewarded with early success. In 1927 he founded *Arts & Métiers Graphiques,* the forward-looking and influential periodical which demonstrated his sure touch not only in type design but also in many diverse fields of art.

After the second world war he played an important role in the development and marketing of the new Lumitype photosetting equipment (known in the US as Photon). Deberny & Peignot acquired the European rights for this equipment and made discs and typefaces for it, ensuring that the company was in the forefront of the many technical changes in typesetting which were to follow.

In 1952 he brought in the Swiss designer Adrian FRUTIGER, then at the beginning of his career as an art director and type designer. The association was a very successful one and among the many new typefaces created in this period are Meridién and Univers.

Charles Peignot was extremely active in the cause of type-

ace copyright and helped found the Association Typographique Internationale (ATypI). He became its first president in 1957, a position which he retained until he was
succeeded by John Dreyfus in 1968. Charles' son, Remy was a
type designer and designed Cristal, a titling face, in 1957.

Deberny & Peignot continued in business until 1972 when
it was acquired by the Swiss typefoundry HAAS.

RCE

John PETERS   1917–89   GB

Angelus (1953)
Castellar (1957) **392**
Fleet Titling (1967) **388**
Traveller (1964)

John Peters worked for University Printing House at Cambridge as a book designer. He undertook several type design
commissions for English Monotype and later founded his
own private press, The Vine Press.

The son of a Member of Parliament and doctor at Law,
Peters began reading architecture at Cambridge in 1936, but
after two years he left the university to join the RAF where he
was commissioned some months before the outbreak of war
in 1939. Shot down over France in 1940 during a reconnais-
sance flight he was seriously wounded (a circumstance which
was to cause him distress later) but carried on with many
more missions with Bomber Command and as a training offi-
cer before leaving the service in 1945.

After a short spell with the Arts Council he married Margaret Shand of the family that controlled Simson Shand and
the Shenval Press. He joined the family firm but soon fell out
with his father-in-law and went to Cambridge University Press
in 1950.

In 1953, with John Dreyfus, he created the typeface
Angelus for a pocket edition of the bible which the University Press planned but never produced. For English Monotype,
where John Dreyfus had become type director, he designed
the titling fonts Castellar, Fleet Titling (intended for use with
the book types Plantin and Ehrhardt), and Traveller (for the
British Transport Commission, although it was never used by
them).

With his friend Peter Foster he set up the Vine Press in
1956 and designed and produced some notable books on a
hand press. Among these was Sir Herbert Reed's *The Parlia-*

ment of Women (1960) and *Design and Tradition* (1962), the first book to be set commercially in Monotype Octavian, the face designed by Will CARTER and David KINDERSLEY.

His life ended sadly in 1989 when the pain caused by his war injury became too much for him (one leg had already been amputated) and he took his own life by shooting himself.

RCB

Alexander PHEMISTER 1829-1894 GB

Franklin Old Style/Modern Old Style (1852)
Full-Grown
Riverside
Standard
Wilson

Born in Edinburgh, and even as a boy showing unusual aptitude for designing letters, Alexander Phemister was soon apprenticed to the famous Edinburgh punch-cutter William Grandison.

Graduating at the age of 23 he immediately attracted the attention of the Scottish typefounders MILLER & RICHARD with whom he cut several series of romans including Old Style, later versions of which were known as Bookface and Bookprint. It was a type which was widely admired and copied because it overcame what was considered archaic in Caslon. The serifs were more slender and more sharply cut, the stress more vertical, but not abruptly so. Indeed, in the following years the work of Phemister on body-type faces made Miller & Richard famous with English publishers.

In 1861 he went to America and for two years worked for George Bruce's & Co. where he cut several notable romans. But it is with the Dickinson Type Foundry of Boston that he spent the greater part of his career. Founded by Samuel Nelson Dickinson in 1839, this great type foundry was almost completely destroyed by fire in 1872 and in order to completely re-establish the foundry Phemister, who was already an employee, was made a partner. Again working with romans he cut numerous faces including Franklin Old Style which had originally been brought out as Modern Old Style with Miller & Richard.

Alexander Phemister was one of the few punch-cutters of his time who designed and cut his own alphabets. His workmanship was the very finest; his taste exquisite: when a letter left his hand it was always perfect: such was the verdict of his contemporaries.

Towards the end of his career, so great was his assurance that he undertook the bold task of producing a small pica for Cambridge University press from design to completion in 30 days. In a rare and revealing demonstration of professional self-confidence he did not see a proof of the face until the book was printed and bound and a copy placed in his hand by the publisher.

He retired when the Dickinson foundry merged with American Typefounders' in 1891 and died in 1894.

RCE

Joseph W.PHINNEY 1848-1934 USA

Jenson (c.1900) **16**

Joseph W.Phinney worked for The Dickinson Type Foundry in Boston, Mass, where he was responsible for the specimen printing department. When the Dickinson was merged with AMERICAN TYPEFOUNDERS' he continued as a type designer with the new company. He was also instrumental in persuading Robert W.Nelson, also formerly with the Dickinson, to take a leading part at ATF, an action which had a fortunate outcome for the company.

During his career he designed many types including ATF Jenson, which was modelled on MORRIS's Golden Type.

RCE

Frank Hinman PIERPONT 1860-1937 USA

Plantin (1913) **39**

Although American, Frank Hinman Pierpont spent most of his career working for English MONOTYPE as the manager of their Salfords works in Surrey, where he stayed from 1899 until his retirement in 1936. His work lay in adapting existing type designs to suit Monotype machines, but in 1913, he oversaw the design of Plantin, which has been described as one of the greatest of the Monotype recuttings of the classics.

Pierpont served his apprenticeship in America with Pratt & Whitney and had worked in patent law before coming to Europe, where he worked for the Berlin company Typograph AG, a subsidiary of Ludwig Lowe. (The typograph was a slug-casting machine designed to compete with LINOTYPE equipment.) He became managing director before moving to

England in 1899 to help set up a factory for Monotype. He brought a core of four of his ex-Typograph employees with him, including Fritz Steltzer who became head of the drawing office.

With Monotype's technical manager Harold Duncan, Pierpont invented and patented a Monotype punch-cutting machine which worked eight times faster than the BENTON-Waldo machine it replaced, and could be used by semi-skilled operators. Pierpont had become interested in such inventions in his twenties while working for a patent lawyer on the Paige typesetting machine, and between 1900 and 1912 he invented and patented more than a dozen improvements to Monotype machinery.

The typeface Plantin followed MASON's Imprint as one of the first to be specifically designed for mechanical composition. A large-bodied face, Pierpont and Steltzer worked from a face in the 1905 PLANTIN-Moretus specimen (although this face was never used by the great Antwerp printer of that name). Plantin was designed with ink-spread in mind so that it would print well on smooth and coated papers.

It has been said that Pierpont, a founder executive of Monotype with a great deal of influence within the company, saw the appointment of Stanley MORISON as Monotype typographical advisor as a threat to his own authority, and also that where conflict did arise between the two men over a revival it was Pierpont that got his way. Seen in this light the cutting of the 'wrong' Fournier from two trial versions in Morison's absence may not have been an accident.

SR

Lucien PISSARRO   1863-1944   F

Brook Type (1903)

Lucien Pissarro was the eldest son of the painter Camille Pissarro. He came to England from France as a young man and stayed for the rest of his life. He was an outstanding book designer and illustrator, and also achieved distinction as a wood engraver.

Pissarro was a friend of Charles RICKETTS through whom he absorbed some of the mediæval influences which dominated English art at that time, but later he openly rejected many of Ricketts' theories.

In 1894 he founded a private press at Chiswick and named it the Eragny Press after the family home in France. Ricketts allowed him to use Vale Press types for his first books, but in 1903 he designed his own, the Brook Type, named after his house in Hammersmith. A venetian type, Pissarro had a photograph of an incunabula page from which to work. This type shows many of the characteristics of the private press types of the period and was only available in one size, pica. Eventually, after the closure of the Eragny Press, it came into the possession of Cambrige University Press.

RCE

Christopher Plantin.   (Photo: St. Bride Printing Library)

Christopher PLANTIN   d.1589   F

[Plantin (1913)] **39**

Christopher Plantin did not design type but was very interested in its selection. He collected type, punches and matrixes buying from, among others, Guillamme Le Bé, Robert GRANJON and Claude GARAMOND.

Although Christopher Plantin was born in France it is his work in the Netherlands that made him famous. He began his working life as a bookbinder, first in Caen and then in Paris. It was probably during his time in Paris that he learnt how to print.

In 1548/9 he settled in Antwerp and was soon established as one of the foremost north European publishers. The firms of Plantin and ELZEVIR dominated Holland with Plantin taking the southern, Roman Catholic part of the trade and Elzevir dominating the Protestant North.

Plantin had an astonishing 21 presses, printing books on a wide range of subjects but his particular interest was publishing. One of his greatest books was the eight volume *Polyglot Bible* in Armenian, Hebrew, Greek and Latin. His fourth daughter Madeleine, a very learned thirteen year old, helped with the proofs.

Plantin set a fashion for engraved title pages; Peter Paul Rubens was among those who designed these for him. In 1567 Plantin published specimens of his types in the *Index characterum* (the first book of its kind), and in 1570 was appointed court printer to King Philip II of Spain.

In 1583 he left Antwerp as the town was being sacked by Spanish soldiers and took up a job as printer to the university in Leiden but he only stayed away two years. He died in 1589 but the printing equipment remained in the family until 1875 when it was sold to the city and became the Plantin-Moretus Museum

The typeface which bears Plantin's name was designed by F.H.PIERPONT. It is not a true revival but was based on a face in the 1905 Plantin-Moretus specimen.

SR

Friedrich POPPL   1923–82   D

Poppl-Antiqua (1967)
Poppl-Exquisit (1970)
Poppl-Pontiflex (1976-79)

Poppl-Residenz (1977)
Poppl-Laudatio (1983)
Poppl-College
Poppl-Saladin
Poppl-Stretto

Friedrich Poppl's early training was in calligraphy: he studied with Herbert POST and continued his studies at the Wiesbaden College of Arts. His calligraphy became well known in the 1960s when his work was shown in several important exhibitions.

All Poppl's typefaces were commissioned by BERTHOLD at the instigation of its artistic director G.G.LANGE. The first, Poppl-Antiqua is a development from his poster lettering but it was not until Poppl-Pontifex was released in 1976 that he achieved international recognition as a type designer.

SR/RCE

Herbert POST   1903-78   D

Post Antiqua (1932-35)
Post Fraktur (1935)
Post Roman (1937)
Post Mediæval (1951)
Dynamik (1952)
Post-Marcato (1961)

The typefaces of the German type designer Herbert Post were cut and produced by H.BERTHOLD AG of Berlin, and are strongly influenced by calligraphy. They are in the tradition of the Offenbach school but still retain the individuality of their creator. His most successful script is the Post Antiqua, which appeared as a set of capitals in 1932 with lower case in 1939.

Post studied painting and design and also trained as a compositor in local technical schools in Frankfurt and Offenbach before he entered the calligraphy class of Rudolf KOCH at Offenbach. Under Koch's direction he was an outstanding student. In 1926 he was invited to go to Halle where an art school under the direction of Paul Thiersch had been established since 1916. Here Post started a fruitful career as teacher, lettering artist, and printer. He returned to Offenbach in 1950 to teach at the Technical Art School and at the same time started the Herbert Post Press. He later took over the direction of the Munich Meisterschule where he found his most rewarding field of work.

RCE

Edward PRINCE   1846-1923   GB

Undoubtedly the greatest punch-cutter of his generation and arguably one of the greatest punch-cutters of all time, Edward Prince was a central figure in the English private press movement at the turn of the century.

He is best known for his work for William Morris (for whom he cut Golden, Troy and Chaucer), who sought his help at the suggestion of Emery Walker; but by this time he was already a highly respected figure. His achievements read like a catalogue of the private press movement both in Britain and elsewhere; the Kelmscott Press, the Vale Press, the Cranach Press, the Ashendene Press, The Doves Press, the Essex House Press, the Eragny Press, the Merrymount Press and the Zilverdistel Press all employed him as a punch-cutter, as did many leading publishers of the day, among them The Medici Society and Chatto & Windus. The astonishing fact is that during all this activity he was also undertaking work at a much lower aesthetic level in the industry as a practical punch-cutter.

It is difficult to overestimate his contribution to the revival of interest in type design which characterised the period and the brilliance of the achievements of the best of the private presses with which he was so intimately associated.

RCE

David QUAY   b.1947   GB

Bordeaux (1988)
Helicon (1989)
Quay Sans (1990)
Agincourt
Arta
Latino

David Quay studied Graphic design at the Ravensbourne College of Art and Design. After taking his degree he worked in various London design studios as a packaging and graphics designer. He became a freelance designer in 1975, specializing in lettering, logotype and graphic design.

In 1987 he founded David Quay Design, a graphic design studio with particular talents in incorporating lettering and letterform design in award-winning graphic communication.

In addition to ITC, his typefaces are offered in the type libraries of Letraset in England and H.Berthold AG in

Germany. David Quay is also Chairman of Letter Exchange, and is the British representative for the Type Directors' Club of New York. He also teaches and lectures regularly in England and Europe. His typeface Quay Sans is a humanistic face based on traditional Grotesque proportions.

RCE

Paul RAND b.1914 USA

Westinghouse Gothic (1956)
City Medium (1966)

Paul Rand was born in New York City and studied at the Brooklyn Institute of Arts and Sciences and with George Grosz at the Art Students League. Always in the vanguard of design developments, Paul Rand was strongly influenced by the many talented designers who chose to leave Europe and settle in America during the pre-war years. Success came early when, at the age of 23, he became art director for two design-conscious magazines, *Esquire* and *Apparel Arts.*

Both his typeface designs form part of corporate identity programs: Westinghouse Gothic for the Westinghouse Corpotation in 1956 and City Medium for IBM in 1966.

Since 1956 he has taught at Yale where he is currently Professor Emeritus of Graphic Design.

RCE

Will RANSOM 1878-1955 USA

Parsons (1918) **239**

Will Ransom started his career in St Louis, Michigan, as a printer on the *Vancouver Columbian* and studied typography in his spare time. He went to Chicago in 1903 and there started his partnership in the Village Press with Frederic GOUDY.

The Village Press was one of the first private presses in America and was a popular meeting place for a number of important figures in the Chicago art world at that time. Two notable visitors there were 'Oz' COOPER and W.A.DWIGGINS.

He designed the typeface Parsons and some ornaments for AMERICAN TYPEFOUNDERS' in 1918 before moving to the University of Oklahoma Press, taking over the post formerly occupied by P.J.CONKWRIGHT who had left in 1939. He remained there for the next fourteen years.

RCE

Imre REINER   1900-87

Meridian (1927-30)
Corvinus (1929-34)
Gotika (1932)
Floride (1939)
Matura (1939)
Sinfonia/Stradivarius (1945)
Reiner Script (1951)
Reiner Black (1955)
Bazaar (1956)
Mercurius (1957)
London Script (1957)
Pepita (1959)
Contact (1968)

The son of a Polish sculptor, Imre Reiner was a painter, sculptor and water-colourist as well as wood-engraver and type-designer.

Most of his early designs were for BAUER in Stuttgart for whom Ernst SCHNEIDLER, the teacher who introduced Reiner to type design, had also worked. The exception was his first face, Meridian, for Klingspor.

Reiner wrote widely on type design and has described how he left Germany for the United States in 1923 planning to work as a graphic artist and to sell a series of sans serif faces. Sans serif faces had not yet established themselves in America; the market proved hostile and Reiner supported himself by manual work for two years before returning to Europe.

The typeface Corvinus (named after an fifteenth-century Hungarian king), was designed to the same formula as the earlier sans serifs but based on nineteenth-century modern faces.

Many of his typefaces are scripts. These include Matura, Mercurius and Pepita for Monotype, and the sans serif script Contact. Pepita is based on Reiner's own handwriting. London Script was designed for the founders Stephenson Blake.

Reiner was married to Hedwig Reiner, née Bauer, a graphic artist, who studied with him in Stuttgart. She was the co-author with Reiner of *Alphabets and Lettering in Book Art*. Reiner's other writing on type includes *Modern and Historical Typography* (published 1950)

SR

Paul RENNER   1878-1956   D

Futura (1927-30) **254, 502, 526**
Futura Black (1948) **636**
Topic/Steile Futura (1953-55) **614**

Paul Renner, like Jan TSCHICHOLD, wanted types which suited the modern age instead of being revivals from an earlier one. In this, his views were similar to those of the Bauhaus movement whose ideals he shared and influenced without ever being a member.

He established the Meisterschule für Deutchlands Buchdrucker (advanced school of German bookprinting) in Munich and recruited fellow type designers George TRUMP and Jan TSCHICHOLD to teach there. Tschichold was removed from his post and interned by the Nazis for 'subversive typography' in 1933 and Renner himself was forced out in 1937.

His best known typeface, Futura, is the archetypal geometric sans serif. The original design had a lower-case of experimental characters but these were all abandoned before its release by BAUER in 1927. It has proved the most popular of its type, eclipsing the earlier Erbar, and still retains its popularity today.

SR

Paul Renner's original designs for Futura.
(Photo: St. Bride Printing Library)

Charles RICKETTS 1866-1930 GB

Vale Type (1896)
King's Fount (1903)

One of the most important and influential personalities in the Private Press Movement was Charles Ricketts who, with his friend Charles Shannon, founded the Vale Press in 1895, but his chief claim to fame rests on the fact that he was the most significant art nouveau book designer, producing some of the most attractive and readable of all the private press books.

The Vale Press differed from William MORRIS's Kelmscott Press in two important ways. Firstly, the Vale Press never had any presses of its own and instead used jobbing printers for all its work and in this respect it more closely resembled the role of the present day designer/typographer. Secondly, whereas Morris and others in the private Press movement where influenced mostly by mediæval models, Ricketts, although he admired Morris's early work, preferred Renaissance models, in particular those of Aldus MANUTIUS, and did not like the heavily over-decorated pages of the Kelmscott Press. In fact Ricketts greatest contemporary influence was the painter Whistler.

As a type designer Ricketts was less successful. Stanley MORISON described his Vale Type (1896, named after his house in Chelsea) as 'affected', and his King's Fount as 'thoroughly bad'.

RCE

Bruce ROGERS 1870-1957 USA

Montaigne (1902)
Centaur (1914) **19**

Bruce Rogers has two claims to fame: he is regarded as the most accomplished book designer America has yet produced and he designed the JENSON revival Centaur, regarded by many as one of the finest types produced this century.

Born in Linnwood, Indiana, Rogers had an early ambition to be an artist and studied at the nearby Purdue College (now University), where he became aware of fine books. His early commercial work was, like many of his generation, influenced by the works of William MORRIS's Kelmscott Press. He moved to Boston, Mass, in 1895 and there met D.B.Updike, ho introduced him to George Mifflin of the Riverside Press. ogers worked at the Riverside Press until 1911 and estab-shed his reputation as a designer of fine books. His first type esign was based on the type used by Nicolas Jenson for *De raeparatio Evangelica* by Eusebius in 1470, and he suggested s use for the Riverside's forthcoming folio edition of Mon-aigne's *Essays*, hence its name. Although disappointed with he punch-cutter's interpretations of his drawings, it was sat-fying enough for Rogers to decide to give up illustration and ainting and concentrate on typography.

Rogers returned to the Jenson models when twelve years ter he was asked to design a type for the exclusive use of the Ietropolitan Museum in New York. This came much closer to is ideals and it was first used in *The Centaur* by Maurice uerin, published by the Montague Press in 1915.

It was not until 1929 that Centaur became available for achine composition to the printing trade. Rogers super-ised the work, which was undertaken by English MONOTYPE hile Rogers was working in England from 1917 to 1919. Dur-g his stay, a critical report Rogers prepared for Cambridge niversity on the use of type in the university press led to heir eventual appointment of a type consultant: Stanley IORISON.

Rogers' book designs include Morison's essay on *Fra Luca de acioli*, the Italian writing master, but his masterpiece is the *xford Lectern Bible,* which is set in 22pt Centaur and took six ears to produce, finally being published in 1935.

SR

Adolf RUSCH 15thC D

dolf Rusch of Strassburg was a fifteenth-century printer who s thought to be the first printer to design and use a type ased on the handwriting preferred by Italian scholars at that ime as opposed to the Gothic, or black-letter, type which was he usual type used in northern Europe in the fifteenth cen-ury. In one of his books set in the 'roman' type a handwrit-en note indicates that the book was purchased in 1464, that s, one year before SCH-WEYNHEIM & PANNARTZ set up their ress at Subiaco, near Rome, and started printing using a type which was also based on the Renaissance hand.

Rusch, the son-in-law of the first printer at Strassburg, ohann Metelin, was sometimes known as the 'R' printer be-ause of the unusual form of the 'R' in his roman font. RCE

Rudolph RUZICKA, 1883-1978 CS

Fairfield (1939-49) **158**

Rudolph Ruzicka was an engraver and etcher working in wood and copper who produced some notable colour wood engravings; he was also an outstandingly versatile typographer, type designer and book designer.

Born in Czechoslovakia (then Bohemia) he went to Chicago in 1894 and studied at the Chicago Art Institute and three years later was apprenticed to a wood-engraver. In 1903 he went to New York and worked for the American Banknote Company and studied at the New York School of Art. He worked for the Calkins and Holden advertising agency from 1906 but opened his own wood-engraving and print shop four years later.

He worked for Mergenthaler LINOTYPE under Chauncey H GRIFFITH and designed the typeface Fairfield in 1940; when he redesigned the Harvard Business Review in 1953, he used the typeface throughout. He was also the designer and typographer for the 54-volume Britannica series, *Great Books of the Western World*.

During a long association with the printer and historian D.B.Updike, Ruzicka was responsible for designing the annual keepsakes for Updike's Merrymount Press for a number of years.

RCH

Rosemary SASSOON b.1931 GB

Sassoon Family: infant, primary type, primary script (1990-91)

The author of many books on aspects of lettering and handwriting, Rosemary Sassoon first trained as a classical scribe under M.C.Oliver, and much of her early work concerned the devising of methods of teaching lettering. She diversified into studying handwriting and was awarded a PhD by the University of Reading for her work on *The effects of different models and methods on how children learn to write*. This educational work led to research into what kind of spacing children find easiest to read. As a result of these findings she began to develop a family of typefaces first for reading and then for bridging the gap between reading and writing.

Her work has always been that of a designer directed at perceived needs, and she feels strongly that type designers

ave a responsibility to research and consider the specific
equirements of various groups of readers and writers.

The characteristics of all three typefaces in the Sassoon
amily are the baseline exits that contribute to letterspacing
nd identification, and the extended ascenders and descen-
ers that accentuate word shape. A set of cursive faces is
eing prepared which will enable users to be flexible about
he amount of joining they require, it is this flexibility which
ifferentiates this type family from traditional faces.

PB

Friedrich Hermann Ernst SCHNEIDLER
1882-1956   D

Deutsch Römisch (1926)
Kontrast (1930)
Grafik (1934)
Schneidler Mediæval (1936)
Legend (1937)
Zentenar Book & Fraktur (1937-390
Amalthea (1956)
Schneidler Old Style/Bauer Text **14, 17**

riedrich Hermann Ernst Schneidler worked for the BAUER
oundry at Stuttgart and designed a number of elegant type-
aces in the years leading up to World War II. He was also a
eacher at the Stuttgart Academy of Fine Art from 1921 to
949 where he had a important influence on many young
esigners who were to distinguish themselves as type design-
rs in later years, including Imre REINER and George TRUMP.
s a teacher of lettering he was a strong advocate of the study
f other graphic disciplines as an aid to type design.

His private press in Stuttgart was the Junipererus Presse
vhich operated from 1921 to 1925 and produced some fifteen
ooks.

His best known typefaces are Schneidler Mediæval and
egend, issued in 1936 and 1937, both cut by the Bauer
oundry. Amalthea is the italic version of Schneidler
Mediæval and was not issued until the year of his death in
956.

Another typeface created in the 30s was Schneidler
Antiqua, which remained uncut because of the outbreak of
var in 1939, although it is now being revived by Cynthia
HOLLANDSWORTH of Agfa COMPUGRAPHIC.

RCE

Peter SCHOEFFER, see GUTENBERG

SCHWEYNHEIM & PANNARTZ 15thC D

Subiaco (1902)

In 1465 the first press to be set up in Italy was at the Benedictine monastery of Subiaco, near Rome, where two Germans, Conrad Schweynheim and Arnold Pannartz, began printing using a type which has become known as the Subiaco type which was quite different to the Gothic black letter type. It has been described as the first roman type, but some scholars refer to it as a fere-humanistica with roman elements, and it may well have been an attempt to comple ment the humanistic, Renaissance, hand then in favour with Italian scholars, who were, of course, the principle market for the press.

In 1467 the press was moved to Rome and the type was modified and a purely roman type was used. When the first press was started in France in 1470, at the Sorbonne in Paris, the type used was modelled on this later type rather than the black letter then in favour in northern Europe, and until that time the only type known. Because the new type was associated with Rome it was called 'roman', the name still used to the present day.

However, there is some evidence to indicate that the first roman type may have been created some time before 1465 by the printer Adolf RUSCH of Strassburg.

A revival of the Subiaco type was cut by Edward PRINCE for the Ashendene Press in 1902, it is now in the possession of the Cambridge University Press

RCI

Kurt SCHWITTERS 1887-1948 D

Single alphabet phonetic type (1927)

The German Kurt Schwitters is best known as a painter and creator of Merz (collages), but he was also a typographer and type designer, an area in which he was to greatly influence the Bauhaus movement through his work with El Lissitsky and others in the constructivist movement.

He was born in Hanover and attended the Dresden Kunstakadamie for six years, where his influences were

Chagall, Kandinsky and Rembrandt. From 1915 onwards he began to develop MERZ, his own new form of artistic expression, collage, and assemblage of art and non-art. Merz was used as a description for all subsequent work—Merz-painting, Merz-writing, &c. In 1924 he set up his own advertising and design agency, Merz-Werbenzentral, and between 1923 and 1932 published *Merz,* a magazine which became an important vehicle for the work of artists such as Mondrian and El Lissitsky. His own most important work at this time was the progressive conversion of his Hanover house into a strange three-dimensional collage which he called the Merzbau, described by Max Ernst as 'a huge abstract grotto'

His one typeface proposal dates from 1927, and like Herbert BAYER's, it was a single alphabet type, but because of his interest in poetry, sound and repetition (a book of his poems *Der Ararat II* had been published in 1924) his was a phonetic version.

Schwitters fled to Norway in 1937 after his work had been included in the Nazi 'Degenerate Art' exhibition. In 1940 he fled to Britain and died in the Lake District in 1948. He was buried in Ambleside, but in 1970 his remains were exhumed and returned to Hanover at the request of his son.

RCE

Erik SPIEKERMANN b.1947 D

Berliner Grotesk (adaptation)
Lo Type (adaptation)
Officina (1990)
Meta (1991)

Erik Spiekermann is an accomplished type designer, graphic designer and typographic consultant. A native of Germany, he spent five years working and lecturing in London and now lives in Berlin, where his studio, MetaDesign, specializes in corporate design work and complex design systems. He is also a principle of the FontShop, a company dedicated to selling high quality PostScript fonts from all the major manufacturers. In addition, FontShop, through its subsidiary FontFonts International, creates and promotes new fonts from up-and-coming designers, and publishes the quarterly disc-only magazine' *Fuse.*

Spiekermann's many type designs include several text faces for Berthold AG and others for private corporate accounts. His typeface Officina, for ITC, was originally conceived as a bridge between old-fashioned typewriter fonts and a traditional typographic design. The object was to produce a type family ideally suited to the multiple tasks of office correspondence and business documentation. His most recent design, Meta, is in part a reaction to the standard corporate typeface Helvetica and in part, an answer to the demands of poor quality papers.

Spiekermann is a frequent writer on type and typography. His best known book is *Rhyme & Reason: A Typographical Novel*, which has been published in German and English.

RCB

STEPHENSON BLAKE & CO.   GB

The original Caslon foundry at Chiswell Street, in which William Caslon III had sold his interest to his mother and sister-in-law in 1792, remained in the family until 1937, but the Caslon foundry in Salisbury Square, originally the Joseph JACKSON foundry, was sold to Blake, Garnett & Co. in 1819, and the entire stock of this famous foundry was removed to new premises in Sheffield. The three original partners in this venture were William Garnet, a silversmith who had worked for Bower & Bacon, a local firm of typefounders, John Stephenson, a toolmaker, and James Blake, a successful filemaker who put up the capital.

During the years preceding this event the Salisbury Square foundry had in fact experienced a complete revival, and between 1807 and 1819, under William Caslon IV, a great variety of new faces had been produced, as can be seen in the sample book issued in the year of the sale. Out had gone the

From Blake, Garnett & Co., *Specimen of printing types,* c.1819.
(Photo: St. Bride Printing Library)

elegant old style letters and orientals; in had come the fat faced romans and much else besides.

John Stephenson was the driving force at the Sheffield foundry and he was a man of great energy, practical skill and taste. He brought a new vigour to the business and between 1820 and 1830 the company flourished with many supplementary specimens being issued. William Garnet withdrew from the business in 1829 to become a farmer and shortly afterwards James Blake died. By 1840 John Stephenson was in effective control of the business as the managing partner with two of the heirs of the Blake family, Thomas Blake and William Thompson. Another partner at this time was W.B.Smith the London representative.

In 1841 the foundry adopted the name by which it is known today, Stephenson Blake & Co., and by this time it can be said that it was on an equal footing with the major London foundries of the day. In the following years the foundry was completely modernised with the installation of many new machines and at The Great Exhibition of 1851 the foundry won a gold medal.

John Stephenson continued to direct the work until 1860, but before his retirement in 1863 and his death a year later, he passed the management of the foundry to his son Henry (later Sir Henry) Stephenson. Under the new partnership of Sir Henry Stephenson, W.G.Blake, and, later, Henry Kenyon Stephenson, the firm continued to flourish, successfully withstanding the major challenge to the typefounding industry posed by automatic typecasting during the latter years of the nineteenth century. Stephenson Blake always remained one step ahead of imitators, particularly in the supply of 'fancy' type and new faces, an area in which they had few competitors but many imitators.

In 1904 Sir Henry Stephenson and Major W.G.Blake both died and control of the business came into the hands of their respective sons, Sir H.K.Stephenson and Robert Greaves Blake.

A year later, as a result of the difficulties experienced by many of the long-established foundries, the company acquired the Fann Street foundry which had started at Nevil's Court and had belonged, in succession, to Thomas Cottrell, Robert Thorne, William Thorowgood, Robert Besley, Benjamin Fox and Sir Charles Reed. Included in the stock of this historic foundry were the old matrices which Dr Fry had bought at the sale of the John Bell types in 1782.

This unique collection of early types was further supplemented by the acquisition in 1937 of the original matrices of the Caslon foundry at Chiswell Street, and in 1952 some of the old MILLER & RICHARD faces were also acquired. Thus, by degrees, Stephenson Blake became the owners of most of the surviving early English and Scottish types; a remarkable collection including Caslon Old Face, cut about 1725; Grove's Union Pearl of 1690, the earliest known decorated type for which the original matrices survive; Thorowgood Italic; Fry's Sans Serifs Shaded; and many more.

Today, the foundry still operates in Sheffield and is the only independent typefoundry in the country. Although a limited company since 1914, it is still a family firm with representatives of both families on the board, every one a practical typefounder.

RCE

Reynolds STONE   1909-79   GB

Minerva (1954)
Janet

Named after his ancestor, the painter Sir Joshua Reynolds, Reynolds Stone is primarily known as an engraver whose work is characterised by a white line on a black background. His work included postage stamps, notes for the Royal Mint, headings for the *Penguin Four Gospels* and many coats of arms. He also cut the Memorials to Sir Winston Churchill and T.S.Eliot in Westminster Abbey.

He was influenced by the Cancellersca style of the sixteenth century Italian writing masters; and by the work of Eric GILL whose pupil he briefly was. He was encouraged to take up engraving and from 1934 he concentrated on woodcutting. In the same year he produced a book, *Lettering*.

Stone's Minerva was commissioned by LINOTYPE as a display face to accompany Gill's typeface Pilgrim (originally known as Bunyan). In addition to Minerva, Stone designed Janet for his own use. This private face was called after his wife, born Janet Woods, whom he married in 1938.

SR

Sumner STONE   b.1945   USA

Stone Family (1987)

Sumner Stone is Director of Typography at Adobe Systems Incorporated in California. At college he studied mathematics and calligraphy (learning the latter from the calligrapher Lloyd Reynolds in Oregon). He has worked as lettering artist for Hallmark Cards but joined ADOBE in 1984. Adobe are the originators of the computer language PostScript and it was for Adobe he designed Stone.

The Stone type family, or 'type clan' as Sumner Stone calls it, consists of three matched types, a roman, a san serif and an 'informal', each in three weights and with an italic in each weight. Stone informal is intended for personal correspondence and similar uses. It is a rounded face with serifs, is of relatively even weight and has some calligraphic features such as the single-bowled a.

Book designer Bob Ishi helped to develop the Stone family, the title of which is actually taken from both men's names; 'Ishi' means Stone in Japanese.

SR

Bradbury THOMPSON b.1911 USA

Monoalphabet (1945, seven experiments)
Alphabet 26 (1950-60)

Bradbury Thompson became designer and editor of *Westvaco Inspirations* in 1939, the house journal of the Westvaco Corporation, the international paper manufacturer. During the next 24 years he made it the most influential and radical publications of its kind. As a vehicle for experimentation in graphic design, and especially typography, it was the perfect tool for his vivid imagination and daring ideas.

His two major contributions to type design are the Monoalphabet, and Alphabet 26. The monoalphabet was based around the thinking of Herbert BAYER, whose famous dictum was: 'Why should we print with two alphabets? Both a large and a small sign are not necessary to indicate a single sound'. Using Futura as the base font Thompson conducted a series of seven experiments introducing a number of variations on this theme with the object, among other things, of improving legibility. It was a subject which was to occupy his mind over a period of over 40 years.

Alphabet 26 originated with his own experiences in teaching his son to read, which led to the conclusion that it is much easier to learn 26 letters than it is to learn 45. The logical conclusion therefore was to choose from the available upper and lower case letters a selection of 26 which would serve both functions with the same form:a natural case in point is the letter 'O'. Alphabet 26 was eventually cut and cast by Lanston Montype, using Baskerville as the base font.

Bradbury Thompson has been a senior critic and visiting professor at Yale since 1953 and is a consultant to Harvard and Cornell Universities and Oxford University Press.

RCE

Robert THORNE 1754–1820 GB

Thorne Shaded (c.1810, re-issued 1936) **402**
Thorowgood (c.1820, revived 1954) **441**

William THOROWGOOD d.1877 GB

Sans Serif Shaded (c.1830, re-issued 1948)

& Benjamin FOX d.1877 GB

the first Clarendon, (c.1845)

Quousque tandem abutere Catilina, patientia nostra? quamdiu nos etiam furor iste tuus eludet? quem ad finem sese effrenata jactabit audacia? nihilne te nocturnum præsidium palatii, nihil consensus bonorum omnium, nihil hic munitissimus habendi senatus locus, nihil horum ora vultusque moverunt? patere tua consilia non sentis? constrictam jam omnium horum conscientia teneri conjurationem tuam non vides? quid proxima, quid superiore nocte ABCDEFGHIJKLMNOPQRST UVWXYZÆŒ œ £1234567890

Robert Thorne: Great Primer No.1 from his *Type specimen book* of 1803. (Photo: St. Bride Printing Library)

In the first half of the nineteenth century, London was at the forefront of typographical innovation, and of the London foundries none was more prominent than that of Robert Thorne.

In 1794 Robert Thorne acquired the London foundry of the late Thomas Cottrell in Nevil's Court. Thorne had been an apprentice to Cottrell, and Cottrell had worked for the first CASLON at Chiswell Street at the same time as Joseph JACKSON. Thorne moved the foundry from Nevil's Court to No. 11 Barbican and within a few years had disposed of most of the old Cottrell stock in favour of types resembling those of Jackson and FIGGINS. His specimen book of 1798 shows a series of graceful romans and italics which excelled those of all his competitors for lightness and uniformity. He also produced some fat-face jobbing letters which were unique at the time for their boldness, and their introduction is judged to have entirely changed the appearance of posters of the period.

In 1802 the foundry was moved once again, this time to the site of an old brewery in Fann Street, Alder's Gate, and the foundry became known as the Fann Street Foundry. It was at this time that Thorne started to produce his self-styled 'improved printing types' which were in fact the first recorded examples of 'modern' faces. With strong vertical colour and fine, horizontal, bracketed serifs they were unique and distinctive and were an immediate success, so much so that Thorne found himself in the vanguard of a new fashion and his style was followed universally by nearly all typefounders.

In the next ten years the foundry saw the addition of many new faces. His fat-face display types were particulary admired abroad, and in 1818 Thorne was paid the signal honour of receiving a commission from the Imprimerie Royale in Paris for cutting fat faces of this kind—which was at that time the only recorded instance of this august institution seeking the advice of a foreigner.

The fat faces were peculiarly English and have been described by Stanley MORISON as the ugliest letters ever cut. However they undoubtedly ministered to the needs of the Industrial Revolution in the production of bold, black letters for all sorts of commercial purposes.

Thorne continued working until his death in 1820 because he was unable to dispose of the foundry to his fellow founders. The Fann Street Foundry was put up for auction in that year and was purchased by William THOROWGOOD with the proceeds—so it was said—of a lucky draw in a state lottery.

Thorowgood came from Staffordshire and had been in the pump business but had no previous connection with type-founding. Despite this not inconsiderable disadvantage he threw himself into the business with great energy and very quickly established himself. Within a few months he brought out his first specimen book which for the most part consisted of the stock as Robert Thorne left it. In the following year he brought out a Greek which was the only learned language type in the foundry at that time, but during the next seven years he introduced Greek, Hebrew, and Russian faces as well as three Frakturs.

When Edmond FRY MD, Joseph FRY's son, retired in 1828 Thorowgood purchased his foundry in Type Street (now Moore Street) and was thus able to make many important additions to the stock, including many oriental and learned faces as well as book founts, blacks, titling and flowers. In 1838 Robert Besley became a partner in the firm and when Thorowgood retired in 1849 the company was renamed R. Besley & Co. Besley's partner was Benjamin Fox, an exceptionally gifted punch-cutter who cut the original Clarendon series, basically an Egyptian with bracketed serifs. Clarendon was extremely popular because it met the demand for a compact dictionary type, an application for which it is still used to this day. Fox went on to cut the Mediæval series, a revival of MILLER & RICHARD's Old Style which proved popular as an alternative to the romans of Isaac Moore and Joseph FRY. He died in 1877, and the stock of the foundry was eventually purchased by STEPHENSON BLAKE in 1905.

RCE

ENGLISH CLARENDON.

Quousque tandem abutere, Catilina, patientia nostra? quamdiu nos etiam furor iste tuus eludet? quem ad finem sese effrenata jactabit audacia? nihilne te nocturnum præsidium palatii, nihil urbis vigiliæ, nihil timor populi, nihil consensus bonorum omnium, nihil hic munitissimus habendi senatus locus, nihil horum ora vultusque moverunt? patere tua consilia non sentis? constrictam jam omnium horum conscientia teneri conjurationem

NUMBER OF MEMBERS, 1,234,567,890.

REMARKABLE MAGNANIMITY. SINGULAR PHENOMENON.

Thorowgood's Clarendon from his *Specimen of printing types,* 1843. (Photo: St. Bride Printing Library)

Walter TIEMANN 1876-1951 D

Tiemann Mediæval (1909)
Tiemann (1923) **159**
Orpheus (1928)
Daphnis (1931)
Offizin (1952)

Walter Tiemann was one of the most important book design-ers and type designers of his generation. In 1906, with his friend Carl Ernst Poeschel, he founded the first private press in Germany, the Janus Press.

Over a period of 30 years he produced sixteen typefaces for the Klingspor foundry in Offenbach, where he was chief out-side designer during the time that Rudolf Koch was its resi-dent type designer.

For many years he lectured at the Staatliche Akademie für Graphische Kunst und Buchgewerbe (State Academy for Graphic Arts and Book Trades) in Leipzig and in 1920 he became its director.

RCE

Walter TRACY b.1914 GB

Jubilee (1954)
Adsans (1959) **249**
Maximus (1967)
Telegraph Modern (1969)
Times Europa (1972)
Telegraph Newface Bold (1989, with Shelley Winter)
Qadi (1979)
Kufics (1980)
Oasis (1985)
Sharif (1989)
Malik (1988)
Medina (1989)

For thirty years Walter Tracy was manager of typeface devel-opment for Linotype in the UK where he created many news-paper text faces and was also responsible for the first major typeface development programme for the composition of Arabic in electronic typesetting systems.

From 1928 he trained as a compositor with William Clowes but soon moved on to typography working first in the typographic studio of Barnard Press from 1935 to 1938 and then, from 1938 to 1946, with Notley Advertising. By 1947 he had become a freelance designer and was quickly recruited by James Shand to work part-time with Robert Harling on the influential publishing venture *Art & Technics*, which specialised in inexpensive books on art and architecture and also produced the journal *Alphabet and Image*.

His first involvement with Linotype came when he was engaged to write and design *Linotype Matrix*, a typographical journal issued by the English Linotype Company, and in 1948 he joined the staff of Linotype as manager of the company's typeface development programme, a job which he retained until 1978.

With Linotype he developed the newspaper text faces Jubilee, Telegraph Modern and Times-Europa, as well as the faces designed for classified advertising work, Adsans and Maximus. His outstanding work in this field earned him the appointment as Royal Designer for Industry in 1973.

In later years he has pursued his special interest in the design of Arabic typefaces designing six since his retirement in 1978. He is the author of two books: *Letters of Credit: a view of type design*, and *The Typographic Scene*.

RCE

George TRUMP   1896-1985   D

City (1930) **192**
Trump Deutsch (1935)
Schadow (Antiqua) (1938-52) **203**
Amati (1951)
Delphin I & II (1951-55) **344**
Codex (1954-6) **334,**
Trump Mediæval (1954-60) **44**
Signum (1955)
Palomba (1955)
Time (1956)
Jaguar (1967)
Mauritius (1968)

George Trump was a teacher of graphics and a type designer with a particular interest in scripts. He designed his types for the Weber foundry in Stuttgart.

While a student at the Stuttgart School he studied under the type designer Professor F.H.Ernst SCHNEIDLER and in 1929 Trump became a lecturer alongside Jan TSCHICHOLD at The Advanced School of Book Printing in Berlin at the invitation of its director Paul RENNER who had seen some of his work at an exhibition in Cologne. Trump left the School to become Director of the School of Arts & Crafts in Berlin but in 1937 was to return, this time as Director, when Renner was fired for 'subversive' typography and arranged for Trump to re-place him. It was at this time that Trump began working for Weber.

Trump had fought in World War I and was called up again in 1939. In 1945 he was badly wounded in the stomach and in 1953 he retired from teaching as a result of his injuries but continued to design type. His major work was the old face type family, Trump Mediæval.

SR

Jan TSCHICHOLD   1902-74   D

Zeus (1931)
Transito (1930)
Saskia (1932)
Sabon (1964-67) **88**

Jan Tschichold was the best known publicist and practitioner of the 'new typography' that developed in Europe between the wars. He has been described as 'the Johnny Apple-seed of typography who carried far and wide the seeds planted in Weimar, Dessau, and Berlin'. He advocated asymmetric lay-outs and sans serif typefaces and rejected revivals of historic styles of type as 'fancy dress'. Later in his career he was to revise such pronouncements, finding them too doctrinaire. Tschichold designed only one widely used type, Sabon, but designed many books and was responsible for establishing design guidelines for Penguin Books.

Tschichold, whose father was a sign-painter, was born in Leipzig and spent the greater part of his teenage years study-ing calligraphy, typography and engraving, initially on his own but later, from 1919, at the Academy for Graphic Arts and Book Trades in Leipzig and at the School of Arts & Crafts in Dresden. He became a convert to the new style of typography when he visited the Bauhaus Exhibition at Weimar in 1923, but prior to this his work was influenced by Italian Renais-sance types and by black-letter. He was given a teaching post by the Director of the Leipzig Academy, the type designer Wal-ter TIEMANN, and stayed there until 1926. The first of his con-troversial writings on typography appeared in a special edition of a printing trade journal *Typographische Mitteilungen* in October 1925 (El Lissitzky and BAYER were among the other contributors). It was reprinted as a book, *Elementare Typographie,* and was his first written protest against the undisciplined German typography of the period.

From 1926-33 Tschichold taught at the German School for Master Printers in Munich that had been founded by Paul RENNER. Both men were forced out of their posts when the National Socialists came to power, Tschichold being the first to go. Before managing to leave Germany for Switzerland he and his wife Edith were interned, he for six weeks, she more briefly. (In 1954 Tschichold would be invited back to Munich as the school's director, an invitation which he declined.)

It was in 1928, while he was still in Munich, that Tschichold wrote *Die Neue Typographie,* which was aimed at the whole of the printing trade; as Ruari McLean has pointed out in his book on Tschichold: he was capable of relating the ideas of the Bauhaus and the modernist movement in art to ordinary printing. In 1935, while living in Basle, Switzerland, Tschichold published *Typographische Gestaltung (Asymmetric Typography).* In it he criticized centred typography as being too inflexible and in conflict with the requirement that the form of a page of type should suit its function. His writings at this point all advocated exclusive use of sans serif types as the type of the present, asymmetric arrangements and ranged left text, and contrast as a major element in design.

Tschichold is known to have designed more than a dozen typefaces while in Germany in the 1920s and early 1930s, most of which have since been lost. Of those that exist, Transito, is a display face; Saskia, a stencil; and Zeus is a calligraphic sans serif. Much time elapsed before he designed Sabon in the early 1960s at the request of a group of German printers. These printers wanted a GARAMOND-derived type that could be set in foundry type, on MONOTYPE or LINOTYPE machines, and always look the same on the page. Tschichold met this exacting specification with remarkable success and called his type after a Lyon punch-cutter, Jacob Sabon, who is said to have brought the Garamond matrices to Frankfurt.

Jan Tschichold's work, well known among typographers on the Continent, was slow to make itself felt in English-speaking countries. The publishers Lund Humphries did organise a small London exhibition of his work in 1935 and he designed the 1938 *Penrose Annual* for them, but with these exceptions he did not achieve worldwide recognition until after the end of his new typography period. Long before the ime the English edition of his *Asymmetric Typography* appeared in 1967, Tschichold had decided that there was a place for symmetrical typography after all: indeed many of his own designs for books used centred text. His chief work in Switzerland was book design: the two main publishers he worked for were Benno Schwabe & Co and Birkhauser.

Tschichold's work for Penguin was done between 1947 and 1949. He was invited to England by the Director of the Company Allen Lane. Tschichold drew up rigorous guidelines for all Penguin typography; produced a new design for the standard Penguin paperback and also established styles for special series such as the Penguin Poets. He laid out many King Penguins himself.

In 1958 the Institute of Graphic Arts in New York presented him with their Gold Medal and in 1965 the Royal Society of Arts made him the first Honorary Royal Designer for Industry. Tschichold died in Switzerland in 1974.

SR

Carol TWOMBLY 20thC USA

Mirarae (1984)
Charlemagne (1990)
Lithos (1990)
Trajan (1990)

Carol Twombly studied design at the Rhode Island School of Design where she became interested in type design and typography. She received an MS from Stanford University in the graduate programme of Digital Typography under Charles BIGELOW, and later joined the Bigelow & Holmes Studio. In the Morisawa Typeface Design Competition in 1984 she won first prize for Mirarae, a latin design which has since been licensed and released.

Carol Twombly has been with ADOBE since 1988 during which time she has designed Trajan, Charlemagne and Lithos, the first three display typefaces in the Adobe Originals library.

RCE

Gerard UNGER   b.1942   NL

Demos (1976)
Praxis (1977)
Flora (1980)
Hollander (1983)
Swift (1985)
Amerigo (1987)
Orander (1987)
Cyrano (1989),
Argo (in preparation)

Born in Arnhem, the Netherlands, Gerard Unger studied at the Rietveld Academy in Amsterdam from 1963 to 1967. He worked in an advertising agency under Wim CROUWEL and later at Jon Enschedé en Zonen before becoming a freelance designer and typographic consultant. He has produced lettering for signs on the Amsterdam Metro, and typefaces for several manufacturers.

His typefaces up to 1989 were designed for the German company Hell for use exclusively on their machines, with the result that his work was not widely known. Since their release in PostScript format he is now receiving acclaim as one of the leading, living type designers, and his related typefaces Demos (roman), Praxis (sans) and Flora (sloped roman) can be seen as forerunners of Bigelow & Holmes' Lucida, Sumner STONE's Stone and Otl AICHER's Rotis. The body text of this book is set in Swift, designed originally to bring æsthetic qualities to the rigorous demands of newspaper typesetting.

In addition, he is an expert on the history of Dutch Chocolate Letters, a traditional part of the St. Nicholas Day celebrations in the Netherlands. At present he lectures at the Rietveld Academy and operates as a freelance designer.

RCE

Johann Friedrich UNGER   1753-1804   D

Johann Friedrich Unger enjoyed the distinction of holding the sole agency for DIDOT types in Germany, and as a printer he was therefore the first in Germany to use the Didot roman but it is for his attempts to reform the Fraktur that he is cheifly remembered.

After starting his career as a wood-cutter, Johann Friedrich Unger went to Berlin in 1780 and set up in business as a printer. At that time German printing had fallen into decline, part y as a result of the closure of the Luther foundry at Frank-urt, which had done so much to secure the popularity of the GARAMOND and GRANJON designs in the previous two cen-uries. Within ten years Unger had added a foundry to his printing business using some of the matrices which he had acquired from the Luther foundry and also from his friend Firman Didot in Paris.

As a type designer it is mainly with the Fraktur versus Schwabacher debate that Unger was concerned. For some rea-son he had acquired an intense dislike for the inappropriate-ly named Schwabacher, the popular cursive letter which had nothing to do with the little Bavarian town after which it was named, and in 1793 he published his ideas on reforming Frak-tur. At first he had commissioned Firman Didot to re-cut the face but without success. Finally he decided to learn how to cut type himself and eventually, with the help of his assistant, Gubitz, he produced two different designs.

Unger achieved no great success in his day and even now his designs are described as pallid, mainly because he attempted to introduce into Fraktur the lightness of roman models.

However his versions of Fraktur were used for a successful series of pocket editions commissioned by Karl Tauknitz in 1841. A.F.Johnson suggested that by smoothing out the lower case letters of Fraktur he had in fact approached more close-ly the despised design, Schwabach. Despite his attempts Frak-tur, probably the most characteristic of all German typefaces, lingered on in Germany for another half century, albeit part-ly for nationalistic reasons, before being finally overtaken by, of all things, the sans serif.

RCE

Eric VAN BLOKLAND   b.1967   NL
& Just van RUSSUM

Beowolf 21, 22 & 23 (1990)

Born in Holland, Eric van Blokland and Just van Russum both studied at the Royal Academy for Fine & Applied Arts in The Hague and graduated 1989. Both have worked for Eric SPIEK-ERMANN's company MetaDesign in Berlin and van Russum also worked for a time at MONOTYPE in England. They now work in Holland under the group name LetTerRor.

While most typefaces produced on computer aim to imi-tate existing forms, Beowolf, the typeface they have designed,

contains a randomizing element to make it slightly different
each time it is used, descibing it, they have written:

> When you hear someone's voice on the phone and he or she has
> a cold, you can still recognize who is talking. We can recognize
> handwriting, and even decipher how quickly a note was written,
> and sometimes pick up on the state of mind the person was in
> when writing the note. Randomness and change can add new
> dimensions to printwork.

RCE

Cristoffel VAN DIJCK 1601-69 NL

[Van Dijck (1935)] **107**

One of the greatest of all Dutch punch-cutters was Cristoffel
van Dijck (also van Dyck) who was intimately associated with
the golden age of Dutch printing. He became the leading type
founder of Amsterdam in the seventeenth century and his
work did a great deal to establish the reputation of Dutch
types throughout Europe.

Born in Dexheim, Holland, little is known of van Dijck
until he began working as a goldsmith in Amsterdam around
1640. A few years later he set up a typefoundry there and
although he seems to have regarded it as a trade rather than
a creative pursuit his craftsmanship was superb. The great
Dutch publishing house of ELZEVIR used his types to the exclu-
sion of all others and William CASLON is thought to have used
van Dijck's roman as the model for his own.

In 1935 Stanley MORISON commissioned Jan VAN KRIMPEN
to advise on the design of a MONOTYPE version of a van Dijck
type .

Van Dijck died in the winter of 1669/70, as did his contemporary, the great Dutch punch-cutter Bartholomeus VOSKENS.

RCE

Jan VAN KRIMPEN 1892-1958 NL

Lutetia (1925) **25**
Antigone (Greek, 1927)
Open Roman capitals (1929)
Romanée (1928, italic 1949)
Romulus (1931) **105**
Cancelleresca Bastarda (1934) **381**
Van Dijck (1934) **107**
Spectrum (1952) **97**

Sheldon

Jan van Krimpen was a skilled calligrapher but believed calligraphy and type design to be essentially different and his types show little calligraphic influence. His letter forms have been described as 'austerely restrained'. Although beautiful and influential, they are not widely used.

After studying at the Academy of Art in the Hague, Jan van Krimpen worked as a freelance designer and illustrator. At 31 his work was spotted by Dr Johannes Enschedé of Joh. Enschedé en Zohen in Haarlem, who asked him to design a new type for his company. Pleased with the result he invited van Krimpen to join them as one of their house designers. He was to stay with the company until his retirement.

This first van Krimpen type, Lutetia, was cut by P..H. Rädisch and cast at the Enschedé foundry. It made its first appearance in an illustrated summary of Dutch art which Holland entered in the Paris exhibition of 1925, hence its title: Lutetia was the Roman name for Paris.

Enschedé is known for its collection of historic type specimens and van Krimpen designed Romanee to accompany an italic in their possession attributed to VAN DIJCK, Kleine Text Curcyf No.2 of 1768, although van Krimpen doubted the attribution. Stanley MORISON of MONOTYPE was a great admirer of Lutetia and commissioned van Krimpen to work on the revival of Van Dijck. He based the italic on Kleine Text Curcyf No.2 but the roman is based on another Enschedé specimen which appeared to be the work of the same man, and which was first used in a 1671 edition of *Ovid* printed in Amsterdam. Later, Monotype also issued three weights of one of his most original faces, Romulus, originally issued by Enschedé. When originally released it was notable for including three text romans and four mated sans serifs.

Van Krimpen did not confine himself to type design but was also a notable book designer, working for Enschedé and fulfilling commissions from other presses.

In World War II, during the occupation, he developed his last type, Spectrum, originally commissioned by Spectrum Publishing Co but subsequently released by Monotype.

In 1930 he wrote an article *Typography in Holland* for the last issue of the influential type journal *The Fleuron*. He examined his own work in the book *On Designing and Developing Type*.

SR

Bartholomeus VOSKENS   died c.1669   NL

In 1638 Bartholomeus Voskens, a sculptor of Breda, was
admitted to the freedom of the city of Amsterdam. It is possible that this may have been the same Bartholomeus Voskens
who started a typefoundry in Amsterdam in 1641 in partnership with his brother Reinhard. Whatever the case, by 1647
the partnership had dissolved and Bartholomeus, now almost
certainly operating alone, is not heard of until a letter-cutter
and founder of the same name is recorded in Hamburg, 'outside the Schar Gate near the Herren moat'.

It was here that Bartholomeus' only known specimen
sheet was published in about 1665. Showing romans, italics,
frakturs and schwarbachers, as well as Hebrew, Syriac and
Greek fonts, the work is of outstanding quality. Eventually he
returned to Amsterdam where he died in the severe winter of
1669-70.

RCE

Ong Chong WAH   b.1955   MAL

Abadi (1988) **304A**
Footlight (1988)

Born and educated in Malaysia, where English was the lan-
guage of instruction, Ong Chong Wah came to England and
from 1976 to 1980 was formally trained in graphic art at
Sunderland   Polytechnic   and   Newcastle-upon-Tyne
Polytechnic. He then worked as an advertising designer for
the London advertising agency Saatchi & Saatchi Compton.
His two type designs, Footlight and Abadi, were designed for
Monotype.

RCE

Justus Erich WALBAUM   1768-1839 or 1859   D

Walbaum (1919) **161, 167-8, 187**

Justus Erich Walbaum was a German punch-cutter who had
his own letter foundry, first based in Goslar and later in
Weimar. His faces were neo-classical, derived from the DIDOT
roman. The founders Berthold still own his original matrices
which they bought (from F.H.Brockhaus) in 1919.

Walbaum, the son of a clergyman, was born in Steinlah.
He was apprenticed to a confectioner and reputedly taught
himself engraving by making his own confectionary moulds,

using chisels he had made from sword blades. When he was free to leave the pastry shop he got a job engraving music types for the Brunswick firm of Spehr.

He set up his own foundry in Goslar in 1793 but the town was too small for him and in 1802, just before independent imperial Goslar was to be incorporated into Prussia, Walbaum left for Weimar. The foundry he set up there was extremely successful and the types he cut—modelled very closely on Firman Didot's—were much admired. From 1828 onwards, the foundry was managed by his son Theodore and when Theodore died in 1836 Walbaum sold the business to F.H.Brockhaus who moved it to Leipzig. After Walbaum's death, typographic fashion moved away from the classical and his types were ignored.

Walbaum's types became available in Britain through the Curwen Press in 1925 and Monotype Walbaum was cut between 1930 and 1959.

SR

Emery WALKER   1851-1933   GB

Doves Type (1900)
Cranach Press Roman (1913)
Ashendene Press Type
Eragny Press Type
Vale Press Type

& Thomas J.COBDEN-SANDERSON   1840-1922   GB

Emery Walker and Thomas J.Cobden Sanderson made an unlikely but creative partnership of opposites (Fiona MacCarthy, in her book on Eric Gill calls them 'A kind of Laurel and Hardy of fine printing). Unfortunately an initially productive relationship degenerated into bitter quarrels, mainly over Doves, the press's own type, which was used most notably in the *Doves' Bible*.

Emery Walker had a background in commercial printing and process-engraving. On 15 November 1888 he delivered his now famous lecture on typography to the Arts & Crafts Exhibition Society. William MORRIS was present and was inspired to start the Kelmscott Press and asked Walker to become a partner; Walker declined but did become his typographical advisor and helped nurse him during his final illness.

After Morris's death in 1896 he was offered the chance to run the press with Sydney Cockerell but again refused, and in

1901 he set up the Doves Press—named after a local inn—with Thomas J.Cobden-Sanderson, a bookbinder who had also worked for Morris.

Like Morris's Golden, and the types of other private presses of that time, Doves' took a JENSON type as its model, in this case that used in Jenson's Pliny of 1476. It was cut by Morris's punch-cutter Edward PRINCE, and used in the press's first work, the five-volume *Doves' Bible*. Unfortunately each partner claimed authorship for himself and in 1912, as a result of this dispute Cobden-Sanderson threw the matrices and type over Hammersmith Bridge into the River Thames. Emery Walker had left the partnership in 1908.

After this, Emery Walker acted as an advisor for the Ashenden Press, Eragny and Vale Presses and for the Cranach Press in Weimar. With the punch-cutter Edward Prince and the draughtsman Percy Tiffin he produced types for all of them. After producing a roman like the Doves Press type for the Cranach Press in 1913. Kessler found that they were out of their depth with the italic (based on a model by the scribe Tagliente) and at his request it was drawn by Edward JOHNSTON.

Walker and the Cranach Press's owner Count Kessler were consultants to publishers Insel Verlag and recommended Eric GILL (for a while a neighbour of Walker's), Edward Johnston and Graily Hewitt.

Walker sat on many committees (some concerned with his other great interest besides printing, architecture). He helped instigate the teaching of printing at the Central College of Arts & Crafts and in 1927 became President of the Arts & Crafts Exhibition Society. He was on the governing bodies of three art schools, was knighted in 1930 and elected and Honourary Fellow of Jesus College, Cambridge in 1933.

SR

Frederic WARDE   1894-1939   USA

[Arrighi (1925 & 1929)] **379**

Frederic Warde was born Arthur Frederic Ward in Wells, Minnesota. He served in the US Army Air Service between 1917 and 1919. In 1918 he met Beatrice Becker whom he later married. Through Beatrice's mother he got his first job, with the MacMillan Company, then left for the printing house of William Edwin Rudge, with whom he was to maintain a connection for much of his life. He soon became supervisor of

MONOTYPE Composition and received training at the Lanston Monotype Company's School in Philadelphia. In 1922 he was appointed Director of Printing at Princetown University Press. His work was chiefly book design and he established a reputation for himself as an uncompromising perfectionist, and was frequently hard to work with for this reason.

It was during this period that he married Beatrice, then working as assistant librarian at the ATF Library in New Jersey (the librarian being the famous Henry Bullen). Together they organised the exhibition *Survivals in the Art of Fine Printing* at the art museum in Princetown. Frederic wrote, designed and printed the catalogue.

In 1925 they left America for Europe going first to France, where they met Stanley MORISON, and then with him to England. While in England Frederic and Beatrice (she under the name of Paul Beaujon) wrote for *The Fleuron*. It was an article by Paul Beaujon entitled *The 'Garamond' types, sixteenth- and seventeenth-century sources considered* in issue 5, which established her reputation as a type scholar and she is the better known of the couple.

In 1925 Frederic designed Arrighi (also known as Centaur italic), an italic based on the sixteenth century script type. It was cut by Charles Plumet in Paris and first appeared in Robert Bridges' poetry book *The Tapestry*. The following year it was used for the purpose for which it had been designed; in the introduction to *The Calligraphic Models of Ludovico Degli Arrighi*, a complete facsimile of a book by the sixteenth century Roman writing master. The book was printed by Hans MARDERSTEIG of the Officina Bodoni in Switzerland

This first Arrighi italic was revised by Warde and cut by Monotype in 1929 to accompany Bruce ROGERS' Centaur. The two versions differ in the terminals to their ascenders, Monotype's having a horizontal, leftward serif.

After its cutting, Frederic separated from Beatrice and returned to America hoping to find financial stability, but the stock market crash worked against him. He resumed work with William E. Rudge as a book designer until Rudge's death.

SR

Emil Rudolf WEISS   1875-1943   D

Weiss Fraktur (c.1913)
Weiss Antiqua/Weiss Roman (1926-31)
Memphis (1929) **196,456.**
Weiss Rundgotisch (1936)

The German Emil Rudolf Weiss worked all his life in the private press movement and designed hundreds of books, including many for the leading German publishers of the day. His work embraced calligraphy, typography and type design, including roman and fraktur types.

His first study was painting, in his native state of Baden, where he received instruction from Hans Thoma and Leopold von Kalckreuth in Karlsruhe. In Paris he studied at the Julian where one of his fellow students was Toulouse-Lautrec. His first ambition in life however, was to be a poet and in 1894 he sent some of his poems to the literary magazine *Pan* which at that time was edited by Otto Julius Bierbaum. Weiss had a particularly fine writing hand which impressed Bierbaum so much that he asked Weiss to prepare a page of letters for publication in *Pan*. The letters appeared in the following year and were the forerunner of a long and distinguished association with design, typography and calligraphy, an area in which he was largely self taught.

Like many German artists of his generation Weiss was aware of the private press movement in England and greatly admired the work and ideals of William MORRIS. But unlike Morris he did not eschew the mechanical methods of reproduction available at the time and he mainly studied the typefaces of the eighteenth-century masters: Goeschen, UNGER, Breitkopf, WALBAUM, DIDOT and BODONI.

In 1902 he was commissioned by the BAUER foundry to design a Roman typeface, a Fraktur and some ornaments. Weiss Fraktur was issued by the Bauer foundry in 1913 but Weiss Antiqua (Roman) was not completed until 1931. Weiss Fraktur, according to D.B.Updike, was highly considered in Germany because it went some way towards solving the problem of a book type of German script which was agreeable and readable.

In 1923 he went to Spain for three months and summarised his experiences in a book which he wrote, designed and illustrated. Entitled *Three Months in Spain: Drawings and Notes By a Painter*, it is regarded as a classic of book design and an outstanding example of a book as a homogeneous work of art. It is reported that as a calligrapher he had few equals and his etched title pages for several limited editions of the Marees Gesellschaft Sappho are regarded as supreme examples of book art.

RCE

Adrian WILLIAMS   b.1950   GB

Worcester Round (1974)
Raleigh (1977)
Seagull (1978)
Stratford (1978, with Freda Sack)
Claridge (1979)
Congress (1980)
Trieste (1983)
Monkton (1986)
Eurocrat (1987)
Poseidon (1987)
Mercius Types (1988)

Adrian Williams is one of the most prolific type designers of the present generation. Wide-ranging interests and many sources of influence, both in the present and in the past, are demonstrated in his work.

Trained at Hornsey School of Art, his first job was drawing photosetting fonts from manufacturers drawings but he soon set up in business on his own and began designing his own typefaces of which four were released by LINOTYPE.

In 1980 he formed a new company marketing a novel concept called, Club Type. This was an arrangement whereby typesetters would receive original Adrian Williams typefaces at the rate of two six-weight families a year on the basis of a three year membership contract. Today Club Type typefaces are becoming available in PostScript format.

RCE

Alexander WILSON   1714-84
& the Wilson Foundry   GB

Great Primer Greek (1757)
Double Pica Roman (1768)
Fontana (1936, see MARDERSTEIG*)* **65**

In 1742 Alexander Wilson set up a typefoundry in St Andrews, Scotland. This foundry, which later moved to Glasgow, ended the dependence of Scottish printers on types brought in from London and the Netherlands; indeed it was to become a serious rival to London foundries. While Alexander Wilson ran the foundry (originally with a partner, John Baine) it produced types which were influenced by the work of CASLON and BASKERVILLE. Chief among their customers were the Foulis (pronounced 'Fowls') brothers, printers to Glasgow University and famous for their editions of the classics.

Alexander Wilson was born in St. Andrew's but after completing his education left for London in 1737 where he became assistant to a french surgeon and spent his spare time researching both medicine and astronomy.

Curious about all matters technical or scientific, Wilson visited a letter foundry with his friend and fellow Scot John Baine. While there the two men had an idea for improving the process of setting types. They worked on their new method (probably a forerunner of the stereotyping system) and though they could not make it work successfully they did decide to return to their home town of St Andrews and set up a letter foundry in 1742. Two years later they moved to Camlachie near Glasgow. They set up another foundry in Ireland and when the size of this enterprise demanded the full-time presence of one of the men they drew lots, Wilson stayed behind, and Baine went to Ireland.

The Foulis did not use leading for their books, preferring instead long bodied types and these the Wilson Foundry delivered. How many of the types offered by the Wilson foundry were cut by Wilson himself (rather that his partner Baine) is not known. Only one roman and a Greek can be firmly attributed to him but both types are highly acclaimed. The Foulis greatest book, a 1768 quarto edition of *Gray's poems,* uses the roman; a double pica. Their four volume *Homer,* 1756-58, uses the Greek.

In this century English Roman No. 1, a Wilson Foundry type though possibly not designed by Alexander Wilson himself, served as the model for Hans Mardersteig's Fontana, designed for Collins of Glasgow in 1936. The Wilson model was first used in an edition of *Horace* in 1760. Another face still in use, Georgian, has been said to be a product of the Wilson Foundry face but Stanley MORISON discovered it on a specimen of John BELL's where Bell states it was cut for him by Richard Austin. No doubt both foundries' use of Austin's skills explains the Wilson attribution.

By the time Wilson cut the double pica roman, referred to

Alexander Wilson's Greek from Foulis' *Iliad* of 1756.
(Photo: St. Bride Printing Library)

ΙΛΙΑΣ. Η. 470.

Χωρὶς δ' Ἀτρείδησ', Ἀγαμέμνονι καὶ Μενελάῳ,

Δῶκεν Ἰησονίδης ἀγέμεν μέθυ, χίλια μέτρα.

Ἔνθεν ἄρ' οἰνίζονῖο καρηκομόωνῖες Ἀχαιοὶ,

Ἄλλοι μὲν χαλκῷ, ἄλλοι δ' αἴθωνι σιδήρῳ,

Ἄλλοι δὲ ῥινοῖς, ἄλλοι δ' αὐτοῖσι βόεσσιν,

Ἄλλοι δ' ἀνδραπόδεσσι· τίθενῖο δὲ δαῖτα θάλειαν.

Παννύχιοι μὲν ἔπειῖα καρηκομόωνῖες Ἀχαιοὶ

Δαίνυνῖο, Τρῶες δὲ καῖὰ πῖόλιν ἠδ' ἐπίκυροι·

Παννύχιος δέ σφιν κακὰ μήδεῖο μητίεῖα Ζεὺς,

Σμερδαλέα κῖυπέων· τὺς δὲ χλωρὸν δέος ἥρει·

Οἶνον δ' ἐκ δεπάων χαμάδις χέον, ὐδέ τις ἔτλη

Πρὶν πιέειν, πρὶν λεῖψαι ὑπερμενέϊ Κρονίωνι.

Κοιμήσανῖ' ἄρ' ἔπειῖα, καὶ ὕπνυ δῶρον ἔλονῖο.

2 2

above, for the Foulis, his involvement in typefounding was
virtually over since he had been made the first Regia Professor of Practical Astronomy at Glasgow University. In conse-
quence he handed over the running of the foundry to his son
Andrew and grandson Alexander who ran the foundry until
it went bankrupt in 1845, at which point the younger Alexander sold the stock to various foundries, including Caslon and
possibly FIGGINS.

Notable cutters to work for the Wilson foundry include
Richard Austin, who cut a modern face for them, and Johann
Christian BAUER who was later to start his own foundry in
Frankfurt. The Miller Foundry in Edinburgh was started by an

ex-manager of the Wilson foundry and the Wilsons themselves were also later to open an Edinburgh branch (it was here that Johann Bauer trained as a punch-cutter) and Alexander's grandson kept this branch open when he transferred the foundry's main operation to London in 1834).

In keeping with its founder's taste for innovation, the foundry was the first in Britain to try and use a type casting machine and though they failed, Marr, who bought up their Edinburgh branch, modified the method and succeeded.

SR

Shelley WINTER b.1959 GB

Pegasus Bold (1980, with Matthew Carter for Berthold Wolpe)
Mitsubishi Arabic (1987, with Tim Holloway)
New Johnston Signage Light (1988)
Sun Life Engraved (1988)
Telegraph Newface Bold (1989, with Walter Tracy)
Telegraph Newface Roman (1990)

Shelley Winter runs Type Design, an independent consultancy which she established in 1981. She has carried out commissions for major international companies and has worked with some of the leading figures in type design. Her career started in the type development department of LINOTYPE in 1977 where she worked with Walter TRACY in the development of Arabic and Cyrillic typefaces. After leaving Linotype she collaborated with Walter Tracy on Telegraph Newface Bold, the headline face for The Daily Telegraph, and later personally developed Telegraph Newface Roman.

With Matthew Carter she collaborated on the development of foreign characters for his Galliard series and with Berthold Wolpe and Matthew Carter she worked on Pegasus Bold for the Berthold Wolpe 75th birthday tribute at the V&A in 1980. She has been commissioned to design laser fonts for DTP systems and to improve screen fonts on a word processing system for ICL.

RCE

Berthold WOLPE 1905-89 D

Hyperion (1931)
Albertus (1932-40) **218**
Tempest (1935)

Pegasus (1938-39; italic & bold, 1984) **235**
Sachsenwald (1938)
Decorata (1955)
Johnston's Railway Type Italic (1973)

Berthold Wolpe, born in Offenbach near Frankfurt in 1905, spent the greater part of his working life in England. From 1941 to 1975 he designed book-jackets for the publisher Faber & Faber, creating as many as 1,500 designs. His best known type is Albertus which was commissioned by Stanley MORISON of the MONOTYPE Corporation. He was also a teacher of lettering at both Camberwell College of Art and the Royal College of Art, London.

As a young man Berthold Wolpe was apprenticed to a firm of metal workers where he learnt chasing, smithing and engraving skills. During his apprenticeship Wolpe became interested in inscriptional lettering and calligraphy. This led him to study at the Offenbach Technical Institute under the calligrapher and type designer Rudolf KOCH. Koch designed types for the Klingspor foundry and like Wolpe he had come to type designing from a background in metalwork. Wolpe progressed to working as his assistant at the Institute and became a teacher in his own right in 1929. Wolpe's work at the Institute included jewellery and tapestry design.

Rudolf Koch's son, Paul Koch, cut Wolpe's first type in 1932 for the BAUER foundry. Originally called Matthias Claudius but later re-named Hyperion, Bauer did not make it available to the trade until after World War II.

Albertus was commissioned in 1932 while Wolpe was on a visit to England. At Morison's request it was based on lettering he had cut in relief from a metal block. For a time it became the most ubiquitous display typeface in Britain and in 1988 was used by The Corporation of the City of London on all their signing including street names.

In 1935, with Koch's death and the rise of Nazism in Germany, he came back to England to stay. Before joining Faber, Wolpe worked for the Fanfare Press. He designed Tempest Titling for them (cut by Monotype) and some modern printers flowers called Fanfare Ornaments.

Pegasus was another Morison commission, cut by Monotype in 1938 with numerals added the following year. Because it was only cut in one size this book type was used only occasionally, a limited edition of Ted Hughes' *Crow* produced in 1973 being one example. In 1980 Matthew CARTER adapted

Pegasus for filmsetting and in the same year it was used for the catalogue for Wolpe's 75th birthday tribute and retrospective at the Victoria & Albert Museum. In 1984 with the addition of a roman and italic, it was issued by Mergenthaler LINOTYPE for digital setting. Wolpe also designed a romanised blackletter called Sachsenwald in 1937; a set of foliated capitals called Decorata for the Westerham Press in 1955, and in 1973 designed an italic for London Transport to accompany the type designed for them by Edward JOHNSTON in 1916.

Berthold Wolpe was made a Royal Designer for Industry in 1959, an Honorary Doctorate from the Royal College of art in 1968, and was awarded an OBE in 1983. Wolpe had a great number of interests including collecting books and hand-tools. He died in July 1989.

SR

Hermann ZAPF   b.1918   D

Michelangelo (1950)
Palatino (1950) **84**
Sistina (1950)
Melior (1952) **138**
Sapphire (1953) **546**
Virtuosa (1953)
Aldus (1954) **75**
Kompact (1954) **451**
Mergenthaler Antiqua (1954)
Optima (1958) **268**
Venture (1969) **351**
Hunt Roman (1962),
Jeanette (1967)
Firenze (1968)
Textura (1969)
Medici (1969)
Hallmark Uncial (1970)
Missouri (1971)
Scriptura (1972)
Crown (1972)
Orion (1974)
Comenius (1976)
Zapf Book (1976)
Marconi (1976)
Zapf International (1977)

Edison (1978)
Zapf Dingbats (1978)
Zapf Chancery (1979) **316**
Vario (1982)
Aurelia (1983)
Euler (1983)
University of Wisconsin Sequoia (1984-7)
Alkor (a music type)
Gilgengard
Phidias & other Greeks

Hermann Zapf is a prolific type designer and a notable writer on type. He spent the early part of his career working for the Stempel foundry in Germany and his work helped to fill the shortage of designs for roman typefaces that existed in West Germany after the war (the main source of such types, Leipzig, having gone to the East). Since leaving Stempel Zapf has designed typefaces for a number of companies, among them BERTHOLD, ITC, Hell Digiset and Hallmark Cards (for whom he made a film about his work in 1968). Much of his later work has involved creating types for digital setting.

In 1935 Zapf was an apprentice to the printers Karl Ulrich & Co when an exhibition of the work of Rudolf KOCH made him decide to teach himself calligraphy. He used a book of Koch's and one by Edward JOHNSTON and when his apprenticeship came to an end he went to work for Koch in Frankfurt. It was in Frankfurt that Zapf was introduced to the Stempel foundry and he began creating types for them, assisted by their head punch-cutter August Rosenberger. It was in this period that Zapf wrote *Feder und Stickel (Pen and Graver)*, a book of calligraphic alphabets. He finished it in 1941, was then conscripted and worked as a cartographer. While in the army he sketched flowers for what was to become *Das Blumen ABC (The Flower Alphabet)* which Stempel were to issue in 1948. Rosenberger cut the plates for both books.

When Zapf returned from the war he took over the design directorship of Stempel. Although he was to resign this post in 1956 to spend more time on other work this was to be a particularly productive time for him. Zapf faces of this post-war period include Palatino a design based on Renaissance forms which was much admired and quickly issued by other foundries, being an early typeface available in PostScript format it has recently been undergoing something of a revival. He used it for the introduction to *Feder und Stickel* when it was published in 1949. In 1954 another Zapf book was published the first volume of his *Manuale Typographicum,* the second volume of which appeared in 1968.

In 1958 he designed Optima, often referred to as a 'stressed sans' but one which Zapf himself called a 'serifless roman'. It was inspired by inscriptional lettering he had seen in Florence, and has proved especially popular with calligraphers and carvers.

Since leaving Stempel, Zapf has created typefaces for a number of other companies including Berthold, Hell Digiset and ITC. He has designed new faces for film setting and digitisation as well as overseeing the transfer of many his older designs to the new systems. He has worked as a consultant for Mergenthaler LINOTYPE (in which capacity he designed Ventura) and for Hallmark Cards (1967-72). In 1977 he was made Professor of Typographic Computer Programming at the Rochester Institute of Technology in New York.

Hermann Zapf is married to the type designer and lettering artist Gundrun ZAPF-VON HESSE.

SR

Gundrun ZAPF - VON HESSE   b.1918   D

Smaragd (1953)
Ariadne (1954)
Diotima (1954)
Shakespeare (1968)
Norfret (1986)
Carmina (1987)

Gudrun Zapf-von Hesse, married to Hermann ZAPF, is a largely self-taught lettering artist who began by studying bookbinding under Otto Dorfner at Weimar, and worked from the books of Edward JOHNSTON and Rudolf KOCH but later took instruction with Johannes Boehland. She has designed a variety of typefaces issued by Stempel, including Diotima, a light roman, Smaragd, a set of outline capitals with hair-line serifs, and Ariadne, a set of flowing italic initials. Later work includes Norfret for Berthold, and Carmina for Bitstream.

RCE

GLOSSARY OF SOME TECHNICAL TERMS

Although this book is primarily about the people behind the typefaces, a knowledge of at least some of the technical background and the relevant technology is necessary. While it is assumed that most readers will have some of this background knowledge, some definitions which may prove helpful are given below.

For a concise introduction to the changing methods of type production and its effect on the typefaces themselves, chapter 5 of Walter Tracy's *Letters of credit,* is recommended, while a brief overview of post-metal typesetting systems is contained in Lawrence Wallis's *Modern encyclopedia of typefaces 1960-90.*

NAMES IN SMALL CAPS indicate entries in the main directory of this book.
Names in italics refer to other entries in this glossary.

Cathod Ray Tube (CRT): an electronic device used in many of today's *image-setters* to transmit the *digitally*-stored letter images onto the film or paper output.

Clarendon: A design with strokes of almost even weight, characterised by heavy, bracketed serifs. A sub-group, comprising newspaper types, is sometimes referred to as *ionic.* See also historical introduction, p.5.

Classification of typefaces: an attempt has been made in this book to keep within the groups set out in the British Standards Institution guidelines of 1967, which in turn were based on the 1954 Vox system of French typographer

Maximilien Vox. The basic chronology is outlined in the historical introduction.

Cold composition: any method of typesetting which outputs onto sensitised paper or film. Cold composition is also used to describe forms of 'direct' or 'strike-on' typesetting devices such as the IBM 'Selectric'. These are, in effect, electic typewriters with proportional spacing and *fonts* held on interchangeable 'golf-balls'.

Digital: a technology which replaced photographic font negatives from the late 1960s onwards, the type is stored as mathematical formulæ in digital form. See also Foreword, p. vi, and historical introduction, p.7.

Egyptian: Similar to clarendon but without the brackets to the serifs. See also historical introduction, p.5.

Filmsetting: like *photosetting,* this is often used as a blanket term to describe any form of post-metal typesetting. Early systems, introduced from the 1950s onwards, used a negative of the typeface, which was exposed photographically onto film or paper. Today it is usual for the type to be stored as mathematical formulæ in digital form and exposed to the film or paper via a *CRT* or *laser imagesetter.* See also foreword, p. vi, and historical introduction, p.7.

Facsimile: A revival of an existing (usually historic) typeface which takes into account all the imperfections (ink-squash etc.) and idiosyncracies of the original model, rather than regularising them for current taste. Perhaps the best examples of this distinction are Monotype's Poliphilus, a *facsimile,* and Bembo, a *revival.*

Font (US)/fount (GB): originally this describes the quantity of type of a given size required for a job. Strictly speaking, it is not another term for a typeface or design but in common usage it is becoming so, and this is the meaning generally used in this book. The American spelling is used, except when reffering to a specific face, eg: Charles Ricketts' King's Fount.

Grotesque: see *sans serif.*

Hot-metal: type from a *mechanical composition* system.

Ionic: newspaper types like the typeface of the same name. A sub-group in the *clarendon* classification. See also historical introduction, p.5.

Latin: a type having triangular, wedge-shaped *serifs*. It dates— like *clarendons* and *egyptians*—from the nineteenth century.

Linotype: see *mechanical composition*.

Matrix: a brass or copper image of a character from which the (metal) type is cast. Also used to describe the photographic negative used in *photosetting* systems.

Mechanical composition: any form of typesetting system involving a keyboard and a hot-metal caster. Developed from the 1880s on, the two main kinds are best represented by the 'LINE-O-TYPE' and the 'MONO-TYPE'. The Linotype assembled a line of character matrices and cast each line of type as one piece of metal known as a 'slug'. The Monotype cast type as individual characters.

Modern: introduced in the 1780s by Firmin DIDOT and Giovanni Battista BODONI, these types are characterised by a vertical shading and an abrupt change from thick to thin stroke. Influenced by copperplate engraving more than the pen, they seem constructed rather than drawn. See also historical introduction, p.5.

Monotype: see mechanical composition.

Old face/old style: types from c.1465 to c.1725 are refered to as old face and are characterised by a calligraphic, ie oblique, stress. The basic design shows national characteristics hence, Dutch old face, etc. Old style is often used to indicate types designed last century which display old face features, but the two terms are often used interchangably. See also historical introduction, p.4.

Pantograph: a diamond-shaped device of jointed metal rods used to reproduce a drawing at a different scale. Capable of reproducing minute detail, it was adapted by Linn Boyd BENTON in 1885 to cut *punches* mechanically from drawings typically ten inches high. The speed of production of punches, compared to hand punch-cutting, made possible the rapid advancement of *mechanical composition*.

Photosetting: see *filmsetting*.

PostScript: a page description language developed by ADOBE Systems Inc. and introduced from 1983 onwards. It is probably the commonest form of *digital* type and important because it is device and resolution independant: type and images in PostScript format will output on any device with a PostScript interpreter. See also historical introduction, p.7.

Punch/punch-cutter/punch-cutting: of the various skills necessary for the production of metal type, that of the punch-cutter was the only one visible. Put simply, a punch was a short metal bar onto the end of which a character was 'cut', by hand and at the actual size of the required type. When completed, the metal was hardened and stamped into a bar of brass or copper, the matrix: from this the type was cast. Early punch-cutters such as GRIFFO, GARAMOND and FOURNIER cut their own types and were, in our modern sense, designers. Later punch-cutters, such as BASKERVILLE's John Handy, were interpreters. From 1885 onwards, the *pantograph* increasingly took over the punch-cutter's role and the majority of metal types produced this century were cut mechanically, from drawings, by this method.

Re-issue: as opposed to a *revival* or a *facsimile.* An historic type re-issued in its original form and often cast from the same matrices. Many nineteenth-century decorated faces returned to favour in the 1950s and were re-issued.

Resolution: the number of lines per inch at which a particular typesetting system outputs type, or at which the typeface was originally scanned.

Revival: an adaptation of an existing design for newer technology or methods of manufacture. the design may be regularised to some degree, depending on the age of the original. A revision which is pedantic in its retention of all the idiosyncracies of the original is sometimes called a *facsimile.*

Roman: either: upright as opposed to *italic,* the normal weight as opposed to the **bold,** or; a seriffed face as opposed to a sans serif. The meaning is generally clear from the context.

Sans serif: 'without *serifs'.* A useful description only in-so-far as it describes what a typeface is not. Attempts have been made to divide the classification into meaningful subgroups—grotesque, neo-grotesque, humanist, etc.—but none has really caught on. See also historical introduction, p.6.

Serif: the accretion at the end of the stems of roman letters thought by some to originate from stone-carving practice. In extended copy, serifs help knit letters into word shapes and are therefore a considerable aid to legibility.

Size: early printers' type sizes were named after the works in which they were first used—in France there was Augustin and Cicero, and in Britain, pica, brevier and long primer—but each printers' measurement was his own. Standardisation was a long time coming: Fournier's point system was introduced in France in 1737 and the Anglo-American point system in 1872 but the two systems are not related and neither corresponds to metric or imperial measurments. Point sizes quoted in this book are those of the country of origin. A discussion of the suitability, or otherwise, of point systems of measurement for current technology is beyond the scope of these notes.

Transitional: a rather vague term for the types of the mid eighteenth century, which move away from the oblique calligraphic stress of the old face and point the way to the sharply-cut moderns. See also historical introduction, p.4.

TrueType: a page description language recently introduced for use on the Macintosh. Like *PostScript,* it is device independant.

Venetian: a sub-group of old face types which are characterised by a sloping cross-bar on the 'e'. See also historical introduction, p.3.

SUGGESTIONS FOR FURTHER READING

The information which makes up this book has been compiled from numerous sources, the major ones are listed below to encourage further study.

books & catalogues

ABC-XYZapf: fifty years in alphabet design, edited by John Dreyfus & Knut Ertichson. The Wynkyn de Worde Society, London & Bund Deutscher Buchkünstler, Offenbach, 1989

AICHER, Otl, *Typographie*. Druckhaus Maack, 1988

AMSTUTZ, Walter (Ed.), *Who's who in graphic art*. De Clive Press, New York, 1982

BESANT, Walter, *Westminster*. Chatto & Windus, London, 1925

BURKE, Jackson, *In memoriam*.

CARTER, Rob. *American typography today*. Van Nostrand Reinhold, New York, 1989

CARTER, Sebastian. *Twentieth-century type designers*. Trefoil Ltd., London, 1987

CRAWFORD, Alan, *C.R.Ashbee: architect, designer and romantic socialist*. New Haven, Conn., London: Yale University Press, 1985

DIRINGER, David, *The alphabet throughout the ages and in all lands*. Staples Printers Ltd., London, 1953

DREYFUS, John. *Italic quartet. A record of the collaboration between Harry Kessler, Edward Johnston, Emery Walker and Edward Prince in making the Cranoch Press Italic,* University Printing House Cambridge, 1966

FLEISCHMANN, Gerd. (Ed.), *Bauhaus typography.* Marzona, Duseldorf, 1984

FRUTIGER, Adrian, *Type, sign, symbol.* ABC Edition, Zurich, 1980

GOTTSCHALL, Edward M., *Typographic communications today.* MIT Press, Cambridge, Mass., 1989

GOUDY, Frederic W., *The Alphabet and elements of lettering.* Bracken Books: an imprint of Bestseller Publications Ltd., 1989

HUTCHINGS, R.S., *A manual of decorated typefaces.* Cory, Adams & Mackay Ltd., London, 1965

HUTCHINGS, R.S., *The western heritage of type design.* Cory, Adams & Mackay Ltd., London, 1963

JASPERT, W.Pincus; BERRY, W.Turner; & JOHNSON, A.F., *Encyclopedia of type faces.* Blandford Press, London, Fourth edition 1970, reprinted 1991

JOHNSON, A.F., *Type designs: their history and development.* Grafton & Co, London, 1934

KOCH, Paul. *The making of printing types.* The Sign of the Dolphin, London & The Limited Edition Club, New York, 1933

KOCH, Rudolf, *The little ABC book of Rudolf Koch, Das ABC Buchlein.* With a memoir by Fritz Kredel & a preface by Warren Chappel. David R. Godine, Boston, 1976

LAWSON, Alexander, *The Anatomy of a Typeface.* Hamish Hamilton Ltd., London, 1990

LEWIS, John, *Typography design and practice.* Barrie & Jenkins, London, 1977

Linotype Express, Back to the Future: The First Hundred Years. Linotype Limited, 1988

MCMURTRIE, Douglas C., *The book: the story of printing & bookmaking,* Braken Books, an imprint of Bestseller Publications Ltd., 1989

McGREW, Mac, *The Other ATF*. American Typefounders'

McGREW, Mac, *American metal type faces of the twentieth century*. The Myriade Press, 1986

McLEAN, Ruari, *Jan Tschichold: typographer*. Lund Humphries, London, 1975

MEGGS, Philip B., *History of graphic design*. Alan Lane, 1983

MEGGS, Philip B., *Type and image*. Van Norstrand Reinhold, 1989

MENGEL, Willi, *Druckschriften der gegenwart, klassifiziert nach DIN 16518, bearbeitet von Willi Mengel*. Verlag, Stuttgart, Otto Blersch, 1966

MORISON, Stanley, *On type designs past and present*. Ernest Benn Ltd., London, 1962

PERFECT, Christopher & ROOKLEDGE, Gordon. *Rookledge's International type-finder: the essential handbook of typeface recognition and selection*. Sarema Press (Publishers) Ltd., London, Second (revised) edition, 1990.

Printing and the mind of man. F.W.Bridges & Sons Ltd. & The Association of British Manufacturers of Printers' Machinery (Proprietary) Ltd., London, 1963

REED, Talbot Baines. *History of old English Letter Foundries*. (Revised & enlarged by A.F.Johnston), London, Faber & Faber, 1952

SUTTON, James & BARTRAM, Alan, *An atlas of typeforms*. Lund Humphries, London, 1967, reprinted 1990

SUTTON, James & BARTRAM, Alan, *Typefaces for books*. The British Library, London, 1990

TARLING, Alan, *Will Carter, printer: An illustrated study*. Galahad Press, London, 1968

TRACY, Walter, *Letters of credit: a view of type design*, Gordon Fraser, London & Bedford, 1986

TRACY, Walter, *The typographic scene*, Gordon Fraser, London & Bedford, 1986

26 Letters. An Annual and Calendar of 26 Letters of the Roman Alphabet. (An international co-operation of type designers and type manufacturers, printers and typographers), 1989

Twenty years of the F.W.Goudy awards. The Press of the Hood Mountain, Rochester Institute of Technology, 1988

UPDIKE, Daniel Berkeley, *Printing types, their history, forms, and use: a study in survivals.* Harvard University Press, third edition, 1962

WALLIS, Lawrence W., *Modern Encyclopedia of Typefaces.* Lund Humphries, London, 1990

magazines & periodicals

American Book Calendar

American Printer

Baseline

Book Design and Production,

British Printer

Der Polygraph

Emigré

Fine Print

Inland Printer

Journal of the Society of Italic Writing

Ligature

Linotype Matrix

Monotype Newsletter

Monotype Recorder

Printing Review

Private Library

Signature

Small Offset Magazine

The Alpha

The Colophon

The Fleuron

U&lc

TRADEMARKS

PostScript is a trademark of Adobe Systems Inc.

Macintosh, TrueType and *LaserWriter* are trademarks of Apple Corporation Inc.

Letraset and *FontStudio* are trademarks of Esselte Letraset Ltd.

ITC is a trademark of the International Typeface Corporation.

Linotype is a trademark of Linotype AG.

Monotype, Monophoto and *Lasercomp* are trademarks of The Monotype Corporation plc.

In addition many of the typeface names themselves are registered trademarks of their original manufacturers or copyright owners.

Monotype is a registered trademark of The Monotype Corporation plc and is registered United States Patent and Trademark Office and in certain other countries.

Abadi, Albertus, Arial, Monotype Baskerville, Bembo, Monotype Bodoni, Calisto, Cantoria, Castellar, Monotype Century, Monotype Century Schoolbook, Clarion, Ehrhardt, Figaro, Footlight, Monotype Garamond, Gill Sans, Grotesque, Imprint, Joanna, Octavian, Monotype Old English Text, Nimrod, Perpetua, Placard, Plantin, Photina, Rockwell, Monotype Spartan, Times New Roman, Van Dijck and Monotype Walbaum are registered trademarks of The Monotype Corporation plc.

Apollo, Ashley Script, Bell, Bernard, Biffo Script, Binney, Blado, Braggadocio, Calvert, Centaur, Century Old Style, Clarendon, Clearface, Coronet, Dorchester Script, Egyptian Extended, Ellington, Engravers, Engravers Old English, Falstaff, Felix, Festival, Forte, Gloucester Old Style, Monotype Goudy Old Style. Goudy Modern, Headline Bold, Horley Old Style, Imprint, Inflex, Ionic, Italian Old Style, Monotype Janson, Kino, Klang, Matura, Mercurius, Modern, Monoline Script, Neographik, New Berolina, Neographik, New Clarendon, News Gothic, News Plantin, Old Style, Onyx, Palace Script, Pepita, Poliphilus, Runic, Sabon, Scotch Roman, Script Bold, Spectrum, Swing Bold, 20th Century, Typewriter Elite, Typewriter Gothic and Zeitgeist are trademarks of The Monotype Corporation plc.

AUTHORS & EDITORS

Following the family tradition, **Ron Eason** started his career in engineering, but quickly revoked and instead pursued his first love, music. Trained at the Guildhall School of Music in London, he was for some years a professional violinist before turning his attention to writing, the other strong ambition of his life.

He has been involved in writing, publishing and printing for some major international companies, and has worked on the production of books and periodicals with leading British printers, including Westerham Press and the former Gavin Martin Ltd. *'I'm lucky enough to have worked with a few of the finest designers and typographers around'*

He has also published at least one journal...*'and there could always be another'*. Married with two children, he lives in the Surrey countryside.

Born in 1962, **Sarah Rookledge** graduated from Warwick University where she studied Film & Literature. After working for Salisbury Publishing Services Ltd, she entered book publishing with a move to Sarema Press (Publishers) Ltd. and was involved with many of that company's art and design publications including *Design Brief* and writing and editing a series of bulletins on print and graphics. She wrote the type designers' biographies in the revised edition of *Rookledge's International typefinder,* and it was her research for this last project which was to provide the inspiration for this latest book.

She now works as a short-story writer and freelance journalist and lives in London.

Phil Baines (born 1958), has worked as a freelance graphic designer since graduating from the Royal College of Art in 1987, combining this with teaching part-time at Central Saint Martin's College of Art & Design in London.

His clients have included The Monotype Corporation and the Crafts Council of Great Britain and his letterpress work has been exhibited internationally.

Gordon Rookledge, (born 1933), is the founder (1983), and Managing Director of the art and graphic book publishers Sarema Press (Publishers) Ltd.

1954-58: Austin Miles Ltd.; 1958-64: Eros Engraving Ltd.; 1964-68: Westerham Press Ltd.; 1968-91: Gavin Martin Ltd. (founder, Chairman & MD); 1983- KGM Offset Ltd. (founder, Chairman & MD); 1974-84: p/t tutor Royal College of Art; visiting Lecturer Newham College of Technology and Middlesex Polytechnic; 1985-86: proprietor *Design Brief* magazine; 1983: conceived and joint editor of *Rookledge's International Typefinder: the essential handbook of typeface recognition and selection.*

He is on the committee of the Wynkyn de Worde Society; married with three children he lives in both London and Brighton.